Ana-16
2023

Fools Rush In

A Comedy

Kenneth Horne

Samuel French – London
New York – Sydney – Toronto – Hollywood

FOOLS RUSH IN

Produced at the Fortune Theatre, London, WC2, on 2nd
September, 1946, with the following cast of characters:

Millicent, bridesmaid	Jessica Spencer
Mrs Coot, daily woman	Iris Vandeleur
Mrs Mandrake, housekeeper	Josephine Middleton
Angela, Pam's mother	Joyce Barbour
Pam, bride	Glynis Johns
Charles, Angela's fiancé	Hugh Dempster
Paul, uninvited guest	Bernard Lee
Joe, bridegroom	Derek Farr

The play directed by Richard Bird

SYNOPSIS OF SCENES

ACT I	The lounge-hall of Angela Dickson's house at Ilcombe in Kent. A summer morning
ACT II	
SCENE 1	The same. After lunch
SCENE 2	The same. After supper
ACT III	The same. A week later, after supper

ACT I

The lounge-hall of the seventeenth-century house of Angela Dickson at Ilcombe in Kent. It is mid-morning in summer

At L *double-doors open into a porch with an outer door—the main front entrance of the house. Flanking these double-doors are two long, narrow windows. Up* RC *a door lets out direct into a pleasant garden which is also visible through a wide, latticed window set* L *of the door.* R *a door leads to the rest of the house. Down* L *is a wide, stone fireplace containing andirons and unlit logs. In harmony with its beams and panelling, the room is furnished as far as possible with the heavy oak of the period. There is, however, a modern chesterfield* RC, *a large easy chair* LC, *a small upholstered armchair down* L, *and a small upright chair up* L. *Between the fireplace and the double-doors* L *stands a small desk with drawers. This desk bears a telephone and table lamp and is littered with papers, writing materials, etc. At the desk is a double stool. Before the window at back stands a baby grand piano and stool. Under the piano is a small occasional table. In the corner up* R *is a radiogram, and down* R *a small buffet with drinks. On this buffet stands a table lamp and on the wall over it hangs a clock. The whole effect is tasteful, cheerful and very "lived-in"*

The CURTAIN *ascends on an empty stage. On the piano is arranged a typical collection of wedding presents with book-ends and toast-racks very much in predominance. Paper wrappings, string and cardboard boxes, as well as several garments, lie about the floor down stage between the chesterfield and the fireplace and clutter the furniture. A large, battered suitcase and a few periodicals repose on the chesterfield at the* L *end. The general impression of disorder is amplified by the steady ringing of the telephone, punctuated by repeated appeals on the front door bell and knocker. After a considerable pause Millicent enters* R. *She is a pretty girl in her early twenties, an old school friend of Pam. She is a dramatic art student—enthusiastic, outspoken and a bit cranky, but a nice girl. Half-dressed and wearing one shoe she hobbles hurriedly round the room peering into and under furniture. Presently she discovers on the desk what she is looking for—her other shoe—slips it on and runs off again* R *completely disregarding the clamour of bells and knocker. A faintly irritable voice is heard calling*

Angela (*off* R) Answer that telephone, somebody.

Mrs Coot enters up RC *from off* R. *She is the daily woman; elderly, gaunt, disapproving and obstructive. Carrying a bucket and mop, she moves leisurely in and stands surveying the wreckage with a tight-lipped look. On this particular morning Mrs Coot is the only unconcerned member of the household. She crosses above the chesterfield to* C. *Mrs Mandrake enters* R. *Mrs Mandrake—known as Mandy to the family, in which she holds a*

*privileged position—has been "Nanny" successively to the mother and
daughter of the household. She is in her late sixties, a neat little woman,
prim, defeatist, gentle-hearted and genteel. For the occasion she wears a
dress of dark blue printed marocain. She is in a considerable flutter and
looks rather miserable*

Mrs Mandrake (*urgently*) The tele*phone's ringing, Mrs Coot. (*She hurries
across to the desk*)

Mrs Coot (*muttering half audibly*) What do you expect it to do—bark? (*She
puts down her bucket down* C)

Angela (*off; calling*) Mandy!

Mrs Mandrake (*lifting the receiver*) Yes, Miss Angela, I'm ...

Angela (*off; calling*) The phone's ringing.

Mrs Mandrake (*calling*) I know, I'm ... (*Into the phone*) Yes?

Mrs Coot (*muttering resentfully*) 'Taint my place to answer phones.

Mrs Mandrake (*into the phone*) Yes. Oh yes, Mr Atkins. No, she's ...

There is a further summons from the door bell and knocker

(*She starts*) Mrs Coot, *please* answer the door. (*Into the phone*) Yes?—No,
there's nothing the matter. Why do you ask?

Mrs Coot (*rolling her eyes to heaven with a martyred air and moving towards
the door* L *muttering*) I come 'ere to *do*, not answer door bells. (*She leans
her mop against the piano*) What do they think I am—a flunkey? (*She goes
into the porch*)

Mrs Mandrake (*into the phone*) Oh dear!—Oh, how provoking!

Mrs Coot (*reappearing*) It's a parcel. (*She crosses to* C)

Mrs Mandrake Well, bring it in, please.

Mrs Coot 'E wants me to sign.

Mrs Mandrake (*with a note of exasperation*) Then *sign*, Mrs Coot.

Mrs Coot Oh no! You don't catch *me* signin' me name.

Mrs Mandrake (*very harassed*) Oh dear, oh dear! (*Into the phone*) I'm *so*
sorry. ... Yes. ... Well, if one must, one must. ... Yes, I'll tell her. ...
Very well! Yes. ... Good-bye! (*She hangs up*)

Angela (*off; calling*) Pam!

Mrs Mandrake (*moving into the porch*) Really, Mrs Coot!

Mrs Coot (*defensively*) I signed me name once before. And what 'appened?
Got stuck with *Mr* Coot.

Mrs Mandrake reappears with a parcel

Mrs Coot (*muttering*) Why don't they get a seckertary if they want people to
sign things?

Mrs Mandrake (*crossing to* R) One should be prepared to turn one's hand to
anything, Mrs Coot, in the difficult days in which we live in.

Mrs Coot Take more 'n one to clear up this lot. (*She comes down* LC *and
begins laboriously picking up paper, etc., and tucking it under her arm*)

Mrs Mandrake (*at the door* R; *calling*) It's another parcel for Miss Pam.

Angela (*off; calling*) Where *is* she?

Mrs Mandrake (*calling*) I don't *know*, Miss Angela. (*She crosses to the piano
and puts the parcel on the stool*)

Angela (*off; calling*) Millicent!

Millicent (*off; calling*) Yes?

Angela (*off; calling*) Do you know where Pam is?

Millicent (*off; calling*) Haven't seen her for *hours*.

There are exasperated noises from Angela

What?

Angela (*off; calling*) Never mind.

A door slams off R. *Meanwhile Mrs Mandrake, her lips moving silently, stands anxiously counting on her fingers*

Mrs Mandrake Now the first thing to decide is in which *order* to do things in. (*Enumerating on her fingers*) Flowers!—Washing up!—Sir Charles's carnation!—Beds!—Er, find Miss Pam! I suppose *you* don't know where Miss Pam is, Mrs Coot?

Mrs Coot (*still gathering wrappings*) 'Oo me? I got something better to do than spend me time watchin' out for people.

Mrs Mandrake (*moving* RC; *beginning again*) Flowers!—Washing up!—Carnation!—Beds!—Miss Pam!—Er, oh yes—a car! (*She hurries across to the door* R)

Mrs Coot (*muttering*) What do they think I am—a nurse-maid? (*She puts the wrappings in the fireplace*)

Mrs Mandrake (*at the door* R; *calling*) Miss *Angela*! (*She pauses*) Miss *Angela*!

Angela enters up RC *from off* R. *She is an extremely attractive woman in her early forties; but for all her charm and sweetness she is not overburdened with brains. She has an impulsive, erratic and warm heart with temper to match. Her sense of logic is not too well developed and she has more than a tendency to absentmindedness. She is elegantly dressed for her daughter's wedding and carries a suction appliance for clearing drains*

Angela (*entering*) What is it now, Mandy? (*She closes the door*)

Mrs Mandrake (*turning as she hears Angela's voice behind her*) Oh, Miss Angela, the *Red Lion*'s just called to say that we can't have the Daimler.

Angela (*dismayed*) What?

Mrs Coot, at the fireplace, stops her pottering to listen

Mrs Mandrake Its big end's gone. I suppose somebody's taken it.

Angela But what are we to do? We can't *walk*. (*She moves above the chesterfield to* C)

Mrs Mandrake (*following to* RC) He said we must make do with the Austin.

Angela Can we all get *in* the Austin?

Mrs Mandrake Well, let me see, there's (*ticking off on her fingers*) you and Sir Charles, and Miss Millicent and me—that's four—and . . .

Angela (*interrupting*) And the driver. That's five. Will it *hold* five?

Mrs Coot What's the bride goin' on—'er bike?

Angela Of *course*! There's *Pam*! Well, it'll have to make two journeys, that's all. (*She hands the appliance to Mrs Mandrake and moves purposefully to the phone*) Though white ribbon on an Austin Ten does seem rather absurd. Like—like spats on a schoolboy. (*Into the phone*) Ilcombe two-four, please! (*She pauses, waiting*)

Mrs Mandrake crosses to the back of the easy chair

Where *is* that girl? (*Into the phone*) Oh, good-morning, Mr Atkins! This is Mrs Dickson ... yes. About the car, Mr Atkins ...

Mrs Coot (*crossing to* C) Come to think of it, I did see something white in the summer 'ouse.

Angela (*into the phone*) Yes. Yes, but you see ... (*She breaks off and looks up*) In the *summer*house?

Mrs Coot (*uncertainly*) Well, I ...

Angela (*still with the phone to her mouth*) But she can't be out there on a morning like this. It doesn't make sense. ... Oh, *really!* (*She replaces the receiver and hurries across to door up* RC)

Mrs Mandrake follows up RC

Mrs Coot (*muttering*) Lots o' things round 'ere don't make sense. (*She crosses to the fireplace*)

Angela opens the door and looks out, with Mrs Mandrake peering over her shoulder

Angela (*calling*) *Pam!* Is that *you?*—Well, *do* come in, darling, and make yourself useful. (*She turns away from the door, leaving it open*) *Really*, I don't know what's come *over* everybody this morning. (*She comes down to the back of the chesterfield*) Just *look* at this room.

Mrs Mandrake (*emotionally*) Poor lamb! (*She sniffs, fumbles for a handkerchief and dabs at her nose*)

Angela (*moving* C) Mrs Coot, dear, *do* be an angel and get some of the bedrooms done.

Mrs Coot rolls her eyes to heaven, sighs deeply, dumps her collection of wrappings in the easy chair LC *and crosses resentfully to* R

And what's that *awful* old suitcase doing on the chesterfield?

Mrs Mandrake (*with increasing emotion*) It's Miss Pam's. She's got her things in it—with which to go away with. (*She chokes*)

Mrs Coot (*at the door* R; *muttering bitterly*) 'Oly Matrimony!

She exits

Mrs Mandrake She didn't want it touched. She wanted it somewhere handy, so that when it was all over—she could just ... (*She chokes*)

Angela (*coming in front of the chesterfield*) Well, let's put it somewhere a *little* less obtrusive, anyway. (*She lifts the suitcase, glances round for somewhere to put it and catches sight of Mrs Mandrake's woebegone face. She puts the suitcase down again* L *of the bucket down* C *and moves impulsively to Mrs Mandrake*) Mandy dear, *don't* get upset about it. (*She puts an arm about Mrs Mandrake's shoulders and brings her down* LC)

Mrs Mandrake (*crying into her handkerchief*) I brought her up, Miss Angela.

Angela (*soothingly*) I know, I know. And she's a darling and we don't want to lose her. But she's going to be *happy*. It's all for the best.

Mrs Mandrake That's what *your* mother said when *you* got married.

Angela (*disconcerted*) Yes, well—er ... (*She clears her throat and removes her arm from Mrs Mandrake*) Anyway, Mandy dear, you *must* try to be cheerful, if only for Pam's sake. After all, it's *her* day. It doesn't happen twice in a girl's life, does it?

Mrs Mandrake (*more under control*) Your mother said *that*, too.

Angela (*with a touch of severity*) Now stop being *morbid*, Mandy, and at least *try* to be happy, or I shall get cross.

Mrs Mandrake Wild horses couldn't make me happy today, Miss Angela. I couldn't be happy today, not if you *tortured* me.

Angela (*trying to keep her patience*) Listen, Mandy! Heaven knows, *I* should know the pitfalls of marriage if *any*body should. And *I'm* her mother. And if *I* can present a cheerful front, surely *you* can.

Mrs Mandrake (*weeping afresh*) I brought her up.

Angela (*beginning to lose her temper and shaking Mrs Mandrake by the shoulders*) I *know* you brought her up. And you brought *me* up *too*. And if you can't have any consideration for Pam, you might at least consider *my* feelings.

Pam enters up RC *from off* R. *She is a very pretty girl of twenty-one, sweet natured and lovable but, like her mother, lacking in stability and given to emotional upheavals. She wears her wedding-dress and carries a small black book. She looks rather dispirited*

Pam (*halting for a moment in the doorway*) What's up?

Angela (*in a suddenly matter-of-fact voice*) Nothing, dear! Nothing at all! (*Warningly aside to Mrs Mandrake*) Now, Mandy!

Mrs Mandrake keeping her head turned from Pam and with her handkerchief to her mouth, crosses hurriedly to the door R *and exits*

Pam (*shutting the door*) Did you want me?

Angela (*with mock patience*) I suppose you do realize you're being married in about forty-five minutes?

Pam But I'm ready. I've been ready for *hours*. (*She moves into the room*)

Angela (*moving up* L *of the easy chair*) *You* may be, darling, but nobody else is. (*She moves behind the easy chair*)

Pam Can I help that?

Angela Certainly you can help it. (*Looking distractedly round the room*) You can—you can ... Even the breakfast things aren't washed up yet ... Have your flowers come?

Pam Not that I know of. (*She perches gloomily on the* L *arm of the chesterfield*)

Angela (*hurrying to the telephone*) Oh, aren't people *awful* nowadays? (*Into the phone*) Give me—er ... (*She notices Pam's air of dejection and breaks off. She replaces the phone and crosses impulsively to Pam*) What is it, my pet?

Pam Nothing.

Angela You can't tell me, darling. I know that look.

Pam (*hesitating*) Mummy—I'm not sure that I like it. (*She reaches up and clings to Angela*)

Angela (*full of concern*) Like what?

Pam Getting married.

Angela (*hugging Pam*) Oh, bless her!—What's wrong with it?

Pam (*glumly*) It's not what I'd pictured, that's all.

Angela But what *could* you have pictured that hasn't been done? (*She takes in the surroundings with a gesture*)

Pam Oh nothing, Mummy! I don't mean that. But—*you* know—the idea of bridesmaids and presents and wedding-bells, and a general atmosphere of excitement and gaiety and all that—and—and sort of being the centre of things. (*Gulping with self-pity*) I thought it was going to be such fun.

Angela And isn't it?

Pam (*trying not to cry*) Not so far.

Angela You can't expect anything to run smoothly in wartime, you know—or rather in a—in a post-war period.

Pam (*plaintively*) I know, but there's *no* excitement or gaiety—only muddle and flap. And I'm *not* the centre of things. Nobody takes the least notice of me except for Mandy bursting into tears every time she looks at me.

Angela Well, you won't have any more of *that*, dear. I've *spoken* to her about it.

Pam As for my bridesmaid—anybody would think it was *she* who's getting married. She hadn't even time to do me up.

Angela She's an *actress*, Pam. She's bound to dramatize things a *little*.

Pam Even the presents are mostly book-ends.

Angela (*reassuringly*) They'll come in useful, dear. Joe's a *great* reader.

Pam You can't furnish a flat with book-ends and toast-racks ... Joe belongs to a library, anyway.

Angela (*smiling indulgently*) Pam darling, you're over-excited, that's all.

Pam (*quite violently*) I'm *not* over-excited. If there's one thing I'm *not*, it's *that*.

Angela (*soothingly*) Then you're overwrought. (*She gives Pam a comforting squeeze*) Now *try* to keep cheerful, there's a good girl—just a *little* longer and everything will be all right. (*She kisses her*) It'll soon be over now. (*She glances at the clock*) Heavens, look at the time! I *must* get on. (*She begins to move away, then hesitates*) Now, what was I doing?—Oh, yes! (*She hurries to the phone, picks it up and speaks into it*) Ilcombe two-four, please!

Pam (*rising and moving to* LC; *gloomily*) Now I've gone and made it worse by reading this. (*She indicates her little black book*)

Angela What's that, dear? (*In some surprise*) A prayer-book?

Pam (*nodding*) I thought I ought to read through the ceremony. (*She moves* C)

Angela So *that's* what you were doing in the summerhouse! (*She laughs indulgently*) How *sweet*! (*Into the phone*) Oh, good-morning, Mr Atkins! This is Mrs Dickson—yes. About the ... (*Suddenly to Pam*) What do you mean, you've gone and made it worse?

Pam Well, I never read it before and I don't think I quite realized what I was going to be called upon to say.

Angela (*uncomprehendingly*) How do you mean, dear?

Pam It's frightfully momentous, isn't it?

Angela Of course it is. Everybody knows that getting married is no light matter.

Pam (*very worried*) I know, but—this sort of brings it home to you in a way that, that ... (*She breaks off*)

Angela What *are* you talking about?

Pam It's *frightening*, Mummy. (*She sits on the* L *arm of the chesterfield*)

Angela (*replacing the receiver and crossing purposefully to Pam*) What *is* all this nonsense?

Pam I mean—when you analyse it—it's really nothing less than a succession of the most awful oaths.

Angela *Oaths?*

Pam Yes, definite, solemn vows sworn in a church, before an altar, in the presence of a priest.

Angela But—what on *earth* did you expect?

Pam (*plaintively*) I don't *know*. That's just *it*. I've never really *thought* about it.

Angela (*quite severely*) Then you should have done, Pam. It's too bad of you to start a thing like this at (*she glances at the clock*)—at seven minutes to twelve with *nothing* done and *nobody* ready.

Pam (*defensively*) But, Mummy—when somebody comes up to you and says "Will you marry me?" and you say "Yes", *all* you think about is that you love him because he's a pet, and that it would be lovely to belong to him and have a home of your own and babies and people to stay and everything. It never occurs to you that you're letting yourself in for all these appalling undertakings. (*She indicates the prayer-book*)

Angela (*rapidly losing patience*) For heaven's sake, *what* appalling undertakings? All *you've* got to say is "I will".

Pam (*thrusting out the book*) Yes, but look what I've got to say it *to*. Look at *this*, for instance.

Angela makes impatient noises

> (*She ignores Angela's impatience and reads*) "Will thou obey him and serve him, love, honour and keep him in sickness and in health; and forsaking all other, keep thee only unto him, so long as ye both shall live?" (*She looks up*) And I have to say "I will".

Angela Well, you intend to do all that, don't you?

Pam I do at the moment, yes. But how can I answer for what I shall be feeling like in ten or fifteen years?

Angela (*in desperation, moving to the piano and down again to* C) Pam—sometimes I wonder whether you're quite mentally stable. *What on earth* do you expect them to put in the ceremony *instead* of "I will"? "Well, that's the way I feel at the moment", or "Providing he turns out as nice as I think he will", or what? What do you think it would *look* like in *print*?

Pam (*cast down*) I was afraid you wouldn't understand.

Angela (*softening a little*) Believe me, I'm trying my best, darling, but *really* I ... (*She breaks off helplessly*)

Pam (*trying hard to make her meaning clear*) It's just that *this* (*indicating the* *prayer-book*) puts it in a way that seems so—so *fright*fully final. I mean—*this*, for instance. The Minister says it first—and I have to say it after him. (*She reads*) "I, N., take thee, N. to my ..."

Angela (*mystified*) What do you mean, "N. take N."? I'm sure *I* never had that.

Pam (*with a trace of impatience*) It means, whatever your *names* are, Mummy.

Angela Oh!

Pam Listen, now! (*She reads*) "I, Pamela, take thee, Joe, to my wedded husband to have and to hold from this day forward." (*She looks up*) "From this day forward", Mummy!

Angela Well?

Pam Well, think what it *means*. Just *think*! Three hundred and sixty-five days every year "as long as we both shall live".

Angela But, you insane child, surely you must have realized that marriage is normally regarded as a permanency—even if you *had*n't read your prayer-book?

Pam Yes, of course I'd realized it—in a sort of way, but ... (*she breaks off*)

Angela But what?

Pam (*a little haltingly*) Well, I suppose I've always had it at the back of my mind that, that marriage was the sort of thing that—well, if it didn't work out, one could always do—what you did.

Angela (*rather coldly*) I see. (*She moves away to* LC)

Pam (*rising and starting impulsively towards Angela*) Oh, darling, that sounded beastly. I didn't mean to be hurtful.

Angela (*a little stiffly*) Pam, dear, I haven't the slightest intention of being hurt. For one thing, I haven't time. I was just thinking how delighted Joe would be to know that you were already contemplating divorce, that's all.

Pam (*suddenly impatient; turning and crossing below the chesterfield*) Oh Mummy, how *can* you be so ridiculous?

Angela (*moving to* C; *outraged*) Well, I *must* say! You sit and listen for three weeks to your banns being read. Then at the *last* moment you suddenly become entangled with the prayer-book and spend your wedding morning in a state of—of morbid introspection in the summerhouse—and you have the temerity to accuse *me* of being ridiculous.

Pam (*subsiding into the chesterfield*) I'm sorry.

Angela (*moving to upstage* L *of the chesterfield; in a faintly mollified tone*) Well, let us have no more of it, *please*. It's not only unwholesome, it's—it's inconsiderate. (*She crosses to the telephone, lifts the receiver and hesitates*) You see? I've com*pletely* forgotten what I had to ring up about.

Charles passes the window from off L *and enters up* RC. *Sir Charles is an admirable person of some fifty years and many sound qualities. But he is also inclined to be pompous and, though heartily jocular, is entirely lacking in humour. His solid form is clad conventionally for the occasion*

Charles (*loudly*) Morning, Angela!—Morning, Pam! (*He closes the door and then puts his top-hat on the piano*)

Pam ⎤
Angela ⎬ (*together*) ⎨ (*rather wearily*) Good-morning, Charles!
            ⎦   ⎨ Oh Charles, I'm so glad to see you. We're so *dread*fully
                            ⎩ behind. (*She replaces the receiver*)

Charles (*rubbing his hands briskly*) *Right!* What can I do? Clean the silver? Put out the cat? Anything you like!

Angela Well, if you ...

Charles (*coming down* C; *interrupting; to Pam*) So it's here at last, eh?

Angela (*in alarm*) What is?

Charles The happy day!

Angela (*in relief; weakly*) Oh heavens, I thought you meant the car. (*She moves to the fireplace and in a harassed way begins picking up one or two scraps of paper*)

Charles Well, Pam, how are you feeling?

Pam (*with a watery smile*) Oh, I ...

Charles (*interrupting*) *That's* right! (*Admiringly*) I say, doesn't she look stunning? Makes me feel quite proud to be giving her away.

Millicent enters R. *Although now fully and charmingly dressed for her office of bridesmaid, her toilet is evidently not yet complete*

Millicent (*entering precipitately*) Hullo, Sir Charles! (*She crosses to* L *and begins another frenzied search round the room*)

Charles Morning, bridesmaid!

Angela (*after watching Millicent a moment; faintly irritable*) What do you *want*, child?

Millicent Compact!

Charles and Angela—the latter rather impatiently—join momentarily in the search. Meanwhile Pam, sighing deeply, begins again to study her prayerbook. Millicent finds the compact almost at once in the easy chair

(*Flourishing the compact*) I've got it. (*She makes for the door* R *to Charles with an excited grin as she passes him*) Isn't this exciting? (*She rushes out and immediately bobs back again*) Don't worry, Pam. I'm nearly ready.

Millicent exits R

Pam, reacting to this, lifts her head and stares bleakly after Millicent for a moment

Charles (*moving to* L *of the chesterfield*) Nice child, that!

Angela (*trying to attract his notice*) Charles!

Charles (*to Pam*) Known her long?

Pam (*looking up from her book*) Oh, I've ...

Charles (*interrupting*) *Ah* yes, I remember. Old school friend! Went on the stage, didn't she? Well, I always say that ...

Angela (*moving behind the easy chair; interrupting loudly*) *Charles!*

Pam shrugs slightly and goes back to her book

Charles (*turning to Angela*) Yes, my dear?

Angela Charles, *please* get your mind on to realities. Er—what was it I wanted to ask you? Oh yes. Did you remember to see the verger about the muddle over the bells?

Charles I did, and it's all fixed up. (*He moves to Angela*)

Angela We're to *have* bells *before* as *well* as after?

Charles That's the idea.

Angela Oh, I'm so glad. Pam dear, did you hear? You're to have your bells before the ceremony after all. *Pam! (She comes down towards Pam)*

Pam *(looking up abstractedly)* Eh?

Angela *(moving behind the chesterfield)* I say you're to have your ... *(She breaks off)* Look dear, if you *must* read, read *Woman and Home* or *Men Only* or something. *(She leans over, picks up two periodicals and places them invitingly in Pam's lap)*

Charles *(coming to* L *of the chesterfield)* Mind you, it wasn't too easy. Some of the chaps seemed to think they were being put upon. But what with a little judicious—*you* know *(he rubs his thumb against his fingers indicative of baksheesh)*—and pulling a few strings—we finally got them to pull theirs, so to speak; ha-ha! *(He laughs heartily at his own joke)* Got 'em to pull *their* strings. Ha, ha! *(He makes the motions of bell pulling)*

Pam winces visibly. Angela casts an anxious glance at her and moves close to Charles

Angela *(aside)* Charles dear, if you *don't* mind—try not to be *too* cheerful this morning. *(She indicates Pam confidentially)* She's a little ...

Charles *(interrupting loudly)* Nervous, eh? Well, I'm not surprised. After all, it's a big step and there's no going back once you've taken it.

Now Angela winces. Pam glances up with a frightened look, then seems to hunch even further into herself. The telephone bell begins to ring

(Briskly) Now! What was it you wanted me to do?

Angela *(rather taken by surprise)* Erm! Answer that, would you? *(She begins to cross to the door* R*)*

Charles Right! *(He strides to the telephone, grabs it and lets forth a sudden shout)* HULLO! *(He is one of those people who think it necessary to bellow on the phone)*

Pam starts violently and lets out a little cry

Angela *(at the door; jumping simultaneously)* Wha'? Oh! *(Breathing rapidly, with her hand to her bosom, she pauses momentarily to recover)*

Angela exits R

Charles *(meanwhile shouting into the phone)* YES. ... WHO? ... SPEAK UP, I can't HEAR you. ... Mr WHAT? ... ATkins? ... Oh, the *RED LION!* ... OH, yes, I know; you're doing the CAtering. WHO did? ... WHO? ... Oh, DID she? ... WAIT A MINUTE! *(He turns to Pam)* Do you know if your mother wanted the *Red Lion?*

Pam *(who has been flinching nervously at the uproar; wearily)* I don't know *what's* been going on.

Charles *(into the phone)* HOLD ON, WILL YOU? *(He puts the receiver on the desk and hurries across to the door* R*)*

He exits R

Pam, looking a little shaken, is just settling herself to a deeper absorption in her worries, when there is a ring and knock at the front door

Pam (*sighing with a martyred air*) Oh, bother! (*She puts the magazines off her lap and rises*)

Pam crosses L *into the porch*

Mrs Mandrake enters R. *She hurries across to* L *in time to encounter Pam reappearing from the porch and bearing, with a complete absence of interest, a bouquet incased in white paper*

Mrs Mandrake Oh! I was just coming to answer it. (*Pleased*) Oh Miss Pam, your *flowers!*

Pam Uh-huh! (*She tosses them unfeelingly on to the desk and moves up* L *by the piano*)

Mrs Mandrake (*running to retrieve them; in a shocked voice*) Take *care*, dear! (*She picks up the flowers and in doing so notices the telephone lying on the desk*) Now, who could have left that there like that? (*She replaces the receiver and moves behind the easy chair, a little reprovingly*) You know what your dear grandmother used to say about people who ill-treat books and flowers?

Pam (*walking restlessly up and down*) I know *all* the damn silly things Grandmother used to say.

Mrs Mandrake (*shocked*) *Pam*, dear! (*She moves* R *of the easy chair and peers at her anxiously*) Is anything wrong?

Pam (*halting*) I want to talk to you. (*She leads Mrs Mandrake down to the fireplace*)

Mrs Mandrake (*incredulously*) *Talk* to me! You—you don't mean *now*?

Pam I'm worried, Mandy.

Mrs Mandrake (*alarmed*) But dear, you *mus*tn't be worried—not at the *moment*. There's *so* much to do and so little time left in which to do it in.

Pam I know; that's just it. Look, Mandy, I've . . .

Charles enters R

Oh, hell! (*She throws herself petulantly into the armchair down* L)

Mrs Mandrake moves to the piano

Charles (*crossing rapidly to the desk*) No—she didn't seem to want the *Red Lion*. (*He arrives at the phone*) Oh! Somebody's put it back.

Mrs Mandrake puts her hand guiltily to her mouth

That's all right, then.—*Now!* What's next? (*He stands in thought*)

Pam (*sighs deeply; murmuring*) Oh, for pity's sake!

Charles Ah! Buttonhole! Where are the carnations kept? (*He comes down to Pam*)

Pam In the small greenhouse at the end of the garden.

Charles Right! (*He strides up stage to the door* RC)

Pam (*loudly and deliberately*) *Right down* at the *very far end* of the *garden*.

Charles (*halting*) Right down at the . . .? Oh!

He turns to the piano, picks up his top-hat, puts it on and goes out up RC *and off* L

Pam (*at once, rising*) Now, Mandy, listen!

Mrs Mandrake (*imploringly*) Miss Pam—*please!* (*She comes down* C)
Pam (*forcefully*) I *must talk* to you. Now don't argue!
Mrs Mandrake Then let me just . . .
Pam (*moving towards her; interrupting*) *No*. This is more important than *any*thing. Come here!

She pushes the reluctant Mrs Mandrake to the chesterfield, thrusts her into it and sits beside her, on her L. *Mrs Mandrake still clutches the bouquet*

Mandy—you brought me up; you were my nanny?
Mrs Mandrake (*mystified; faintly*) Yes, dear.
Pam And my mother's nanny before me?
Mrs Mandrake Yes.
Pam And you know more about the family than any other living soul?
Mrs Mandrake Oh no, dear! Not more than your mother. If you *really* want to know anything, you should . . .
Pam It's not a bit of good my asking her about this—because I've tried it before—often—and she just shuts up like a clam. (*She pauses*) Mandy—I want to know about my father.
Mrs Mandrake (*in a horrified half-whisper*) Oh, *dear!*
Pam I hardly remember my father, Mandy, and nobody ever mentions him—and almost as long as I can remember, if there's been the slightest reference to him, everything's always gone sort of quiet—as if somebody had said a rude word or something. What kind of man *was* he, Mandy?

Mrs Mandrake is very disturbed. She clutches the bouquet to her bosom and sits rigidly with downcast eyes and averted head

Mrs Mandrake This is your wedding day. It should be a day upon which to think of pleasant things on.
Pam Was he so dreadful?
Mrs Mandrake (*in a low voice*) Your father was a very wicked man, Miss Pam.
Pam What did he do, Mandy? Tell me!
Mrs Mandrake (*with an effort*) He—he was unfaithful to your mother.
Pam Yes—what else?
Mrs Mandrake (*incredulously*) What *else?*
Pam Well, that hardly makes him the sort of monster I've been brought up to think he was. Didn't he knock her about or anything?
Mrs Mandrake (*quite severely*) There is *nothing* worse than infidelity. Haven't you ever read the "Solemnization of Matrimony"?
Pam *Indeed* I have.
Mrs Mandrake "Forsaking all other, keep thee only unto her."
Pam Still—slipping up once doesn't make him a very wicked man, does it?
Mrs Mandrake (*with severe dignity*) I never *said* he slipped up once. Thank God, I don't *know* the number of occasions upon which he slipped up on.
Pam You mean to say he was a libertine, a roué, a—a profligate?
Mrs Mandrake You know quite well I should never *dream* of taking such words into my mouth. I can only say that he was unfaithful to your mother in Paddington, and that I *always* felt he was a man who was not to be trusted in—in that way.

Pam (*in some surprise*) Right from the start?

Mrs Mandrake Right from the start. It was a *great* pity your mother ever married him.

Pam But *why* did you feel that?

Mrs Mandrake (*a little uncertainly*) Anyone with half an *eye* could see what sort of man he was.

Pam That's what I mean—how?

Mrs Mandrake (*at a loss*) How?

Pam Yes—*what* could you see with half an eye?

Mrs Mandrake Well, I . . . One can't always *say* exactly what it is that . . . There are certain things a woman knows by *in*stinct.

Pam Then what went wrong with Mummy's instinct?

Mrs Mandrake (*bewildered*) I don't follow, dear.

Pam If it was so obvious what sort of man he was—why did she marry him?

Mrs Mandrake She was so young.

Pam (*scornfully*) Oh! Mandy.

Mrs Mandrake I mean "young" in the sense that she was still just a little—headstrong.

Pam She still is. Not to say obstinate!

Mrs Mandrake (*severely*) Miss Pam—you must *not* speak of your mother like that.

Pam Did you warn her?

Mrs Mandrake I naturally couldn't tell a girl of her age *why* I thought him undesirable—but I *did* say I didn't think he was Mr Right.

Pam And she told you to mind your own business?

Mrs Mandrake Well . . . (*She breaks off*)

Pam Exactly! Obstinate!

Mrs Mandrake (*suddenly reminiscent*) If *only* your dear grandmother had let me have her tonsils out, that time! I always say there's nothing like tonsils for making people pig-headed.

Pam Did she love him, Mandy?

Mrs Mandrake (*evasively*) I think she was rather—swept off her feet.

Pam What by—passion?

Mrs Mandrake (*indignantly*) Certainly not!

Pam Well, it must have been *some*thing like that. You don't get swept off your feet by personal regard.

Mrs Mandrake (*stiffly*) I would prefer to say that she was in*fat*uated.

Pam What's the difference?

Mrs Mandrake Miss Pam—I will *not* sit here and listen to you accusing your mother of—of passion. (*She makes to rise*)

Pam (*restraining her*) Mandy, you must learn to face facts. Infatuation is essentially physical.

Mrs Mandrake—still clutching the bouquet—emits a gasping noise and tries again to rise

(*Pushing her back again*) No. Sit down! The main thing is this—*you* could see he wasn't the right man for her, and if *she* had had any sense, *she* could have seen it too. Isn't that it?

Mrs Mandrake (*in full agreement with this*) Yes.

Pam Good! (*She rises and moves behind the chesterfield*)
Mrs Mandrake (*hopefully*) Is that all, then? (*She rises*)
Pam Well, there *is* another thing.

Mrs Mandrake sighs and sinks back into the chesterfield

(*Over the back of the chesterfield*) But you may not want to talk about
this—in which case, of course, you needn't.
Mrs Mandrake (*a little resentfully*) I haven't *wanted* to talk about *any* of
it—but I seem to have done so.
Pam Mandy—*you*'ve been married too.
Mrs Mandrake (*after faint pause; in a small voice*) Not for very long, Miss
Pam.
Pam (*kindly*) Why not? I mean—why didn't *yours* last?

Mrs Mandrake remains with bent head in silence

(*Gently urgent*) It might help me a lot to know.

Still silence

Was it—the same sort of thing?
Mrs Mandrake (*in a half-whisper*) Not—not that I'm aware of.
Pam What then? Desertion—cruelty?
Mrs Mandrake Alcohol!
Pam Poor Mandy! Were *you* very young?
Mrs Mandrake Yes, but—I should have known. He was even drunk when
he asked me.
Pam *Oh*, I'm so glad.
Mrs Mandrake (*startled*) Eh?
Pam Thank you for telling me, dear. (*She stoops over the back of the
chesterfield and kisses her lightly on the cheek*)
Mrs Mandrake (*half rising*) Well, is—is *that* all?
Pam Except Mrs Coot! (*She moves to* R *of the chesterfield*)
Mrs Mandrake (*perplexed*) Mrs Coot? (*She sits*)
Pam Yes. I was wondering about her too. *She* had a husband once, didn't
she?
Mrs Mandrake I believe so—yes.
Pam What was it in *his* case, I wonder—women or beer?
Mrs Mandrake As far as I can ascertain—both!
Pam Should *she* have known?
Mrs Mandrake Unquestionably she should. Mr Coot, I understand, was
*ed*ucated at a reformatory.
Pam (*crossing above the chesterfield to* C) Oh—*lovely*!
Mrs Mandrake (*uncomprehendingly*) Pardon?
Pam *Oh*, I'm so relieved. You don't *know* how happy you've made me,
Mandy. (*She clasps her hands in ecstasy, pivots on her heel and goes up
stage*)
Mrs Mandrake (*bewildered*) *I* have?
Pam Yes, *yes*, don't you see? If it was so perfectly apparent to everybody
that Mr Mandrake and Father and Mr Coot were bad eggs—then you

and Mummy and Mrs Coot were just stupid idiots to marry them, and it was nobody's damn silly fault but your own.

Mrs Mandrake (*beginning gaspingly*) I . . .

Pam (*interrupting quite severely*) You had every warning—all the warning in the world—but no—you had to allow yourselves to be blinded by passion.

Mrs Mandrake (*outraged*) I did *not* allow myself to be blinded by passion and—and—and neither did your mother.

Pam Then you were swept off your feet, Mandy dear, and you have nobody to blame but yourselves. (*She moves to the piano stool and sits*) Oh, I'm so glad. (*She begins gently to play something serene and peaceful, e.g. Grieg's "Solveig's Song"*)

Mrs Mandrake (*beginning to get tearful again*) I can only say, Miss Pam, that I haven't the remotest conception of what you're talking of.

Pam (*contentedly*) *I'm* not being swept off my feet. Nobody could accuse *Joe* of being a feet-sweeper, could they?

Mrs Mandrake Mr Joe is a dear, good, kind boy—and I'm sure he'll make you the best of husbands. (*She begins to sniffle*)

Pam (*nodding gravely as she plays*) That's what *I* think—because *I'm* not infatuated. There's nothing like that to warp *my* judgement. If there were anything funny about Joe, I should be able to see it as clearly as anybody else—shouldn't I?

Mrs Mandrake (*weeping gently*) I'm sure you would, dear.

Charles passes the window

Pam's music instantly changes to "The Soldiers of the Queen"

Charles enters up RC *from off* L

Mrs Mandrake makes dithering, ineffectual attempts to compose herself with an inadequate handkerchief

Charles (*crossing to* C *and turning to Pam across the piano; proudly thrusting out his chest, which now bears a white carnation; loudly to top the music*) How's that?

Pam (*loudly*) Terrific!

Angela's irritated voice is heard outside the door R

Angela (*off*) Who on *earth* is that playing the piano?

Angela enters R

Mrs Mandrake is more flustered than ever in her attempts to mop herself up

(*In a disappointed voice*) Pam. (*She moves above the chesterfield*)

Pam stops playing and turn enquiringly

Mandy, what *are* you doing sitting about the place like that? (*She comes round the* L *end of the chesterfield*)

Mrs Mandrake rises hurriedly, sniffing and dabbing at her nose

And I *did* ask you, for *Pam's* sake, not to *do* that. (*Absently she takes the bouquet from Mrs Mandrake*) Did you phone the florist about the bouquet?

Mrs Mandrake (*scuttling for the door* R; *almost inaudibly*) No.

Angela (*crossing to* LC) Then I suppose I shall have to do it myself. (*She tosses the bouquet into the easy chair*)

Mrs Mandrake exits R

(*Distractedly*) Oh *dear*, oh dear! (*She crosses to* R *below the chesterfield*) I do wish people wouldn't get so distraught.

Charles (*coming down* C) How's the time? (*He moves below the chesterfield to look at the clock*)

Angela Don't speak of it, Charles. I daren't even *look* at it.

Charles (*warningly*) Getting on!

Angela (*taking Charles' arm*) Come with me, dear. I want you to *lift* something.

Charles Right!

They move to the door R. *Angela halts*

Charles continues and exits

Angela turns to Pam as if to say something, but checks herself as Pam smiles widely and cheerfully

Angela remains silent and exits looking mistrustfully bewildered

Pam turns back to the piano and begins again, in an indefinite way, to play. After a few moments she drifts into the "Wedding March". There is a knock at the door .

Pam breaks off, rises leisurely, and mooches across L *into the porch*

Paul (*in the porch*) Good-morning!

Pam Good-morning!

Paul Is Mrs Dickson in, please?

Pam (*rather doubtfully*) Well, she's frightfully busy. We've—got a wedding going on.

Paul Yes, I know.

Pam Oh, is it something to do with that?

Paul Yes. Oh, yes.

Pam Well—come in, please!

Pam enters and stands aside by the upstage door

Paul Dickson enters from the porch. He is a good-looking man in his middle forties. His attractive appearance combines with an agile· and humorous mind to make a very engaging personality. But he is not a man to be put upon. He wears a smart lounge suit and carries a felt hat. He crosses Pam and awaits upstage of the easy chair while she closes the doors

(*Coming down* L *of the easy chair*) We're a bit upset—as you *see*. (*She indicates the room*)

Paul Yes, I . . .

They both laugh awkwardly

Pam (*moving round the easy chair to* C, *facing Paul*) Does Mummy—erm—does she know you?

Paul Oh yes—yes, she knows me.

Pam Oh! (*She moves towards the door* R) What name shall I say?

Paul Mr Dickson.

Pam (*halting at* RC; *in surprise*) Dickson? Really? How odd! That's *our* name.

They laugh together again

(*Continuing to the door*) Well, I'll just see if . . .

Paul Thank you!

Pam (*opening the door* R *and calling*) Mummy! (*She pauses*) *Mummy!*

There is no answer. Pam looks back into the room and catches Paul's eye where he stands politely waiting. They both smirk

(*Yelling*) MUMMY!

Mrs Mandrake (*off; calling*) Feeding the hens, dear.

Pam Oh! (*She shuts the door and turns back into the room*) Oh, well—she's sure to be in a minute. People keep on bobbing in and out this morning. Do sit down!

Paul Thank you! (*He looks round for somewhere suitable to sit, sees only the piano stool and diffidently lifts the parcel from it*) Er—may I?

Pam (*going to him*) Of course! (*She takes the parcel from him and moves down* L) You'll excuse me, won't you, while I . . .? (*She indicates the parcel*)

Paul Of course! (*He sits*)

Paul follows Pam's every movement with his eyes. Pam shows that she is conscious of this as she continues to the armchair down L, *sits and begins to undo the parcel*

Millicent enters R

Millicent (*as usual rushing breathlessly in*) Oh, Pam—have you seen my . . . (*She catches sight of Paul, breaks off and brings herself to an abrupt halt*)

Pam Handbag?

Millicent (*staring at Paul*) Yes.

Pam Over there! (*She nods towards the buffet down* R)

Millicent Oh! (*She moves—but more sedately—to the buffet down* R, *picks up her handbag and returns with it to the door* R, *casting, all the way, interested glances at Paul*)

Millicent exits R

Paul Bridesmaid?

Pam (*looking up with a smile*) Yes. (*She meets Paul's steady stare and looks down again*)

Paul Uh-huh!

There is a pause. Conversation is difficult. Pam is struggling with the knot

(*Putting his hand in his pocket and half rising*) Can I—cut that for you?

Pam Oh no, thank you. Mustn't waste string.

Paul sinks back on to his stool and continues gazing at Pam

(*After a pause, looking up; in an interested tone*) Why do you look at me
like that?
Paul Oh, I'm sorry.
Pam (*reassuring him*) Oh no, don't be sorry. I didn't mean that. Everybody
stares at brides. I just thought you might be wondering whether you'd met
me before. *I* was.
Paul Oh, we *have* met.
Pam We have? I *thought* so. Where was it?
Paul Switzerland.
Pam (*trying to recollect*) Switzerland?—Switzerland? (*She remembers*) Oh,
of course! When I was a kid. The time I went away with my cousins. *You*
taught me to ski.
Paul (*smiling*) That's right.
Pam I was—let me see . . .
Paul (*indicating the height of a child of about eleven*) About so high!
Pam Yes—but how extraordinary! *Mummy* will be *thrilled.* (*She rises*)
Paul (*a shade uncertainly*) I hope so.
Pam (*looking at him*) You've changed, though.
Paul (*smiling*) You have, too.
Pam (*with a little laugh*) I expect I have. (*Having now undone the parcel, she
extracts and holds up a toast-rack: with false enthusiasm*) Look! *Is*n't that
nice?
Paul (*politely*) Lovely!

*Pam moves up to the piano, deposits the toast-rack on it and the box and
wrappings on the table underneath. There is a knock and ring at the front door*

Pam Excuse me!

Pam crosses L *into the porch and answers the front door. Mrs Mandrake
enters* R

*Paul absently strikes one or two chords on the piano. His head is turned away·
from Mrs Mandrake*

Mrs Mandrake (*seeing Paul; at once*) Oh, I'm sorry, but we *can't* have the
piano tuned today. There's such a . . .

*Paul turns to her. Mrs Mandrake breaks off with a gasp and stands rooted,
goggling at him and mouthing like a fish*

Paul (*rising and smiling; quietly*) Hullo, Mandy!

*Mrs Mandrake stands for a moment breathing heavily and clutching at her
throat*

Mrs Mandrake Oh, God in heaven! (*She turns and staggers to the door* R)

Mrs Mandrake exits R. *Pam returns from the porch opening a telegram
envelope and glancing at the contents*

Pam (*coming down* L *and tossing the telegram on to the desk*) Aren't people
sweet?

Paul (*sinking back on to his stool; vaguely*) Yes.

Pam (*glancing at the clock; anxiously*) Oh dear, I hope they're going to be ready. It's getting awfully late. What do *you* make the time, Mr Dickson? (*She moves up to the L of the piano*)

Paul (*looking at his watch*) About—er . . .

Pam (*struck by a thought; interrupting*) But your name wasn't Dickson in Switzerland!

Paul No.

Pam It was . . .

Paul Robinson.

Pam Yes.

They both laugh—Pam rather awkwardly

Isn't that rather—odd?

Paul Not at all. I changed it for the occasion.

Pam What occasion?

Paul Meeting you.

Pam (*bewildered*) I'm awfully sorry, but . . .

Paul You see—I knew you were going to be there.

Pam Yes?

Paul So I made it my business to be there too.

Pam Why?

Paul Simply because I wanted to meet you.

Pam (*quite baffled*) But—but in any case . . . (*She breaks off*)

Angela enters R. She is breathing hard and struggling to maintain a cool and dignified exterior. She comes towards the R end of the chesterfield. Mrs Mandrake follows her in, creeps up behind her and stands staring fearfully at Paul over Angela's shoulder

Paul rises and moves a few steps down C. He and Angela stand staring at each other. Pam glances sharply from one to the other

Paul (*in a low voice, humbly*) Good-morning, Angela!

Angela (*who evidently does not quite know how to handle the situation; coldly*) Good-morning!

Paul (*after a slight, awkward pause; coming forward a step, behind the L end of the chesterfield*) Er—how are you?

Angela I'm very well, thank you.

Paul (*uncomfortably*) Everything all right?

Angela It has been—up to the moment.

Mrs Mandrake (*in a half-whisper*) Ask him what he wants.

Angela (*over her shoulder; impatiently*) Go away, Mandy!

Mrs Mandrake retreats a few paces towards the door, but remains. Pam surveys the scene with growing perplexity

(*To Paul*) Perhaps you'll be good enough to say what you want and then go away. We're very busy here.

Pam (*urgently*) Mummy! (*She comes down C*)

Angela (*to Pam*) And *you'd* better go away, dear.

Pam What *is* this?

Paul (*uncomfortably apologetic*) I'm awfully sorry if I've ... (*He breaks off*)

Angela Well, I'm afraid you have. It's *most* inconvenient.

Paul I just thought I'd like to—come to the wedding.

Angela There's nothing to prevent you from going to any wedding, but there's no need to come here.

Pam (*crossing below the chesterfield, to Angela; suspiciously*) You wouldn't talk like that to just anybody.

Angela I'm well aware of that.

Mrs Mandrake (*moving to Angela's elbow*) Tell her to go away again.

Angela (*to Pam*) Do go away, dear.

Pam I *won't* go away. Who *is* this?

Paul I did think, Angela, that today of all days ...

Pam (*interrupting; insistently*) Mummy, *who is* this man?

Mrs Mandrake (*to Angela*) Don't tell her.

Angela I haven't the remotest intention of telling her.

Paul (*getting annoyed*) Don't be so damned idiotic! *Why shouldn't* she know?

Pam (*turning to Paul*) You're my father, aren't you?

Paul (*loudly and irritably*) Yes!

Angela (*in exasperation*) There you are!

Paul (*moving down stage, R of the easy chair; bitterly*) Who else *could* it be, after a reception like that?

Mrs Mandrake (*wailingly*) Oh *dear,* oh dear!

Pam (*staring at Paul wonderingly*) My—father!

Angela (*to Paul*) Well, now that you've got everybody *thoroughly* upset perhaps you'll kindly ...

Pam (*suddenly rounding on Angela; interrupting*) Oh *do* shut up a minute, Mummy!

Angela (*stiffly*) I *beg* your pardon?

Pam Look—I've just met my *father* for the first *time*. It's a—it's a *very* unusual situation. For *goodness* sake give me a chance to *take* it in. (*She crosses to the fireplace*)

Angela (*affronted*) Very well, my dear—*take* it in. You're the one who's getting married—not me. *I'*m in no hurry. Take all the time you want.

Pam moves towards Paul below the easy chair

Mrs Mandrake (*anxiously*) But, Miss Angela ...

Angela (*interrupting irritably*) Go away, Mandy!

Mrs Mandrake again retreats a few steps. Pam stands regarding Paul steadily

Charles enters R

Charles (*moving behind the chesterfield; bustling cheerfully*) Now then! (*He sees Paul*) Oh!

Angela Charles dear, *would* you mind going away for a few minutes? Take a little walk round the garden, would you?

Charles Why? What's up?

Angela Nothing's exactly up, dear, but ...

Pam (*interrupting*) My father's here.

Charles (*stupidly*) Who?

Pam (*loudly*) My *father*!

Charles (*turning to Angela*) Does she mean your—er—your ex—er ... (*He breaks off*)

Angela (*with a trace of irritability*) Of course she does. Who else would her father be likely to be? (*She moves towards Charles behind the chesterfield*)

Charles Oh! (*He moves to Paul*) How d'you do.

Paul (*nodding abruptly*) How d'you do.

Charles Just come down for the—er ... (*He breaks off*)

Paul That's right.

Charles (*disconcerted*) Oh! (*He crosses up stage of Paul to L and comes down to the fireplace*)

Paul (*to Pam; half humorously*) Well?

Pam (*studying Paul*) You're not a *bit* what I expected.

Paul (*with a faint smile*) Oh? What did you expect?

Pam I don't know really. Somebody with a sort of a—*funny* look, I suppose.

Paul (*mystified*) A sort of a funny look?

Pam (*feeling she has said too much*) Yes, but... (*she begins to edge away up stage*)

Paul Why on earth should you think that?

Pam (*airily*) Oh—I just happened to get the idea.

Paul (*insistently*) But you must have had some ...

Pam (*moving up L of the easy chair to the piano; interrupting*) Anyway you haven't, so it doesn't matter, does it? (*Trying to change the subject, she lifts the new toast-rack from the piano and holds it up*) Mummy, did you see the lovely toast-rack that Mrs Bedford ...?

Paul (*turning up to Pam, snatching the toast-rack from her and tossing it into the armchair LC; interrupting forcefully*) Now, look here! If you thought I had a funny look, you must have had some *reason* for doing so—and I want to know *why*.

Pam I just happened to get the impression that you were the sort of person who went round making passes, that's all.

Paul Doing *what*?

Pam You know—at women.—So naturally I pictured you with a kind of leer.

Paul A kind of a *leer*?

Pam (*weakly*) Yes—that's all.

Pam That's *all*? (*He looks at Angela*)

Angela (*faintly on the defensive*) I'm sure *I* never gave her any such impression, Paul.

Pam Not in so many words—no.

Angela Pam, that's *most* unfair. I've always been most *care*ful to avoid any unsavoury references to your father.

Pam I know. That's just it. (*She moves to Angela*)

Angela And I'm quite sure *no*body has *ever* told you that he *leered*.

Pam Oh yes they have. Only this morning ... (*She points to Mrs Mandrake*)

Mrs Mandrake (*interrupting in panic*) I said nothing of the sort, Miss Angela. (*She backs into the doorway R*)

Pam Well, you hinted it.

Paul (*crossing below the chesterfield to Mrs Mandrake; angrily*) Look here! What have you been telling my daughter about me?

Mrs Mandrake (*terror stricken*) I . . . (*She breaks off*)

Angela (*severely*) Mandy!

Mrs Mandrake (*to Angela*) I merely said that—that Mr Paul had—had been disloyal to us.

Pam You said "unfaithful". (*She crosses to the easy chair* LC)

Angela (*moving round to the front of the chesterfield*) Well, he can't deny it either way. (*She sits*)

Paul (*turning to Angela; fiercely*) I most certainly *can* deny it.

Angela Paul—don't be absurd.

Paul I'm *not* being absurd. All I did was to supply you with the necessary evidence. I don't call *that* being unfaithful.

Angela I've no doubt you had a very good time in the process.

Paul (*frantically indignant*) *Well I'm damned!* I'm decent enough to go through all the sordid business of—of messing about in—in Paddington hotels so that *you* can keep the kid (*with a gesture towards Pam*), and *all* the thanks I get is to have my own child's mind poisoned against me.

Pam (*immersed in her own thoughts*) Well, that settles it, anyway. (*She throws the paper from the easy chair on to the floor, picks up the toast-rack and flowers and sits abstractedly in the chair holding them*)

Charles (*deeply uncomfortable; clearing his throat*) Look, I—er . . .

Paul (*beginning to stride about behind the chesterfield, muttering resentfully*) Never leered at anyone in my life.

Charles Aren't we being a bit public about this?

Paul (*rudely*) Nobody asked you to stand there like that, my friend. (*He moves to* C)

Angela (*rising*) How *dare* you walk into my house after sixteen years and start telling people where they may stand?

Paul Well, it's very embarrassing for me to have to parade my private affairs before strangers in this way.

Angela (*in a transport of indignation*) *Strangers!*

Charles (*haughtily*) I happen to be your—Mrs er—this lady's fiancé.

Paul (*halting suddenly and staring at Charles with an insulting suggestion of incredulity*) You mean she's . . . (*He turns to Angela*) You're going to marry him?

Angela (*acidly*) Have you any objection?

Paul (*with a faint shrug*) It's none of *my* business.

Angela (*sarcastically*) Well, I'm relieved to hear that, anyway. For a moment I thought you were going to start interfering with *us too.*

Paul moves R *behind the chesterfield*

Mrs Mandrake (*moving behind Angela and trying to attract her attention*) Miss Angela!

Angela Go away, Mandy!

Mrs Mandrake But—but what did she (*indicating Pam*) mean just now by "*that settles it*"?

Angela (*turning to Pam*) Yes—what *did* you mean?

Pam remains sunk in meditation

(*Crossing to Pam*) *Pam!*

Pam (*coming to*) Eh?

Angela What settles what?

Pam (*a little sadly*) It's off.

Angela What's off?

Pam The wedding.

Angela (*blankly*) I don't think I follow.

Pam (*rising*) Then I'll try to be more explicit, Mummy dear. The marriage which was to have taken place from here this morning, and in which I was to have figured as one of the principals—*is now off.*

Angela *What on* earth are you talking about?

Pam I can't put it any clearer than that. (*She drops the flowers and toast-rack in the easy chair*)

Mrs Mandrake (*to Angela*) She doesn't *mean* it, does she?   .

Pam (*crossing below Angela to* C) I mean it absolutely. I love Joe and I still hope to marry him—but *not* this *morning.*

Mrs Mandrake (*wailingly*) Miss Pam, you mustn't *talk* like that.

Angela You mustn't dear, *really.* You simply mustn't *say* such things with a church-full of people waiting and—and a reception afterwards and . . .

Mrs Mandrake (*interrupting*) And a cake made, and a car coming and—and your bag packed and everything.

Pam (*in a gentler tone*) I'm sorry, Mummy. Believe me, I'm sorry. I know it must be a shock to you after all the trouble you've taken. It's an awful disappointment to me to, but—it's not right to—to rush into these things, is it?

Angela But—but—*rush?* I don't know what you're talking about. You've been *engaged* for eight weeks. (*She moves below the easychair*)

Pam Well, how long did it take you to find out about Father? More than eight weeks, I know.

Paul (*resentfully*) What does she *mean,* "find out about Father"? (*He comes down to* R *of Pam*)

Pam I'm sorry. I shouldn't have put it like that. That sounds as if I believe it, whereas, as a matter of fact, I'm deliberately keeping an open mind about you.

Paul That's awfully decent of you. But what *is* all this about my private life, and what's it got to do with you, anyway?

Angela Exactly! Why should you adopt this extraordinary attitude simply because your father doesn't look as unpleasant as you expected him to?

Pam It's given me a *jolt,* Mummy. There's *nothing* about him that can be seen with half an eye.

Angela (*uncomprehendingly*) Nothing what?

Pam He's a *thoroughly* presentable person—the sort of person *anyone* might marry in good faith. (*Staring at Paul appraisingly*) Isn't he, now? Be honest!

Angela (*reluctantly*) Well—on the face of it, I suppose.

Pam No less presentable than Joe, for instance?

Charles Oo, I don't know about that.

Paul (*to Charles*) Nobody asked you for your opinion.

Charles (*starting forward aggressively*) Now, look here, sir . . .

Angela *Quiet!*

Charles subsides

Pam (*to Paul*) You mustn't mind us discussing you like this Mr—erm—
Father. But it's *so* important.

Paul (*resignedly; sinking into the chesterfield*) Go on! Go on! Don't mind
me. It's quite an experience. (*He settles down to survey the scene with a sort
of fascinated wonder*)

Angela (*to Pam*) Well?

Pam Well—how do I know Joe won't turn out the same way?

Angela You don't. But you must take *some* risks when you get married.

Paul opens his mouth to speak, but gets no opportunity

Charles Marriage is a lottery, my dear. Hah! (*He begins to laugh*)

Angela quells Charles with a glance

Pam Well, I don't intend to take any more risks than are absolutely
necessary. I'll marry Joe. I *want* to marry Joe—but *only* when I've left no
stone unturned to satisfy myself that—that we're suited.

Angela And what happens to everybody's arrangements while you're
turning stones?

Pam I'm sorry, Mummy. I've *said* I'm sorry. But I can't do it until I know
him better. I *can't*. It wouldn't be *right*.

Paul Why didn't you think of all this before?

Pam (*moving to Paul; beginning a full explanation*) Well, you see—I started
reading the Wedding Ceremony and . . .

Angela (*interrupting*) Oh, good heavens, child—don't begin that all over
again. We haven't *time*.

Pam But there's no hurry now. (*She moves forlornly up stage and leans
against the piano*)

Angela (*in an appalled voice*) Pam, you can't *do* this. (*She moves up stage to
Pam*)

Mrs Mandrake It's a *terrible* thing to do.

Pam (*her lower lip beginning to tremble*) I'm sorry, but I can't *help* it.

There is a frustrated silence. Angela shrugs helplessly at Mrs Mandrake

Charles (*suddenly*) Get Joe!

Angela (*clutching at a straw*) Yes. Yes, that's it. (*She hurries to the phone*)
We'll get Joe. (*She lifts the receiver and pauses*) Ilcombe seven-one-seven,
please.

Mrs Mandrake (*wailingly*) Oh, *dear*, oh dear! If only they had let me have
her tonsils out! (*She sinks into the chesterfield and begins to weep and
gently rock herself*)

Angela (*into the phone*) Has Mr Joseph left yet, please? (*Pause*) Could I
speak to him? It's *most* important. . . . I *know* he's getting married—or, at
least . . . Yes, this is Mrs Dickson. (*She waits, drumming impatiently on the
desk*)

Pam (*beginning to cry*) I don't see why you want to drag *him* into it.—*He*
hasn't done anything. (*She makes ineffectual searching movements as if
looking for a handkerchief and finishes up by wiping her eyes on the backs of
her hands*)

There is a knock at the front door

Angela Charles—would you mind?
Charles Certainly!

Charles hurries into the porch and answers the front door

Paul (*taking out his handkerchief*) Here! (*He hands it to Pam over the back of the chesterfield*)

Pam blows her nose loudly

Angela (*into the phone*) Joe—I'm so glad to have caught you. Could you come over a minute, dear? ... No, I mean *now*, be*fore* you go to the church.... No it *won't* do afterwards.... No, no, nothing to worry about; just a little something that's er—that's come up, that's all.... Would you, dear? ... Thank you! It *would* be a help. (*She hangs up*)

Charles enters from the porch

Charles It's the car. (*He closes the door*)
Angela Oh, heavens. (*She crosses to Pam*)

Charles comes down to the fireplace

Mrs Mandrake (*rising; wailing*) Oh, Miss Angela!
Angela Do be quiet, Mandy! (*She brings Pam down* C) Pam, darling, listen! The *car's* here for Mandy and Millicent and me. Now *do* be a good girl and say you'll get in it when it returns for you and Charles. Just this once, dear! *Do!* To please me!
Pam (*crying freely*) I'm not *going*, Mummy.
Mrs Mandrake (*tearfully*) *Please* go and powder your nose, Miss Pam!
Angela (*still imploring*) Yes, dear, try that! I always do if I'm undecided about anything. It's psychological. You can't go looking like that, anyway.
Pam (*blubbering but obstinate*) I'm *not* undecided. (*Loudly*) *I'm not going.*

Mrs Mandrake moves up R *and crosses to the piano*

Angela (*suddenly exasperated again*) Charles—*you* do something! (*She moves to the fireplace*)
Charles (*advancing purposefully below the easy chair*) Now, look here, young woman ...
Paul You keep out of it!
Charles (*to Paul pompously*) This has gone far enough. (*To Pam severely*) You do as your mother tells you and go and powder your nose at once!
Pam (*loudly*) I *won't*!
Paul (*rising; to Charles*) How would you like to mind your own business for a few minutes?
Charles It *is* my business. I'm her prospective stepfather and I've just been invited by her mother to intervene.
Paul (*crossing to Charles*) Well, you're now being invited by her father to keep your nose out of it.
Angela How dare you speak to Charles like that?

Charles (*advancing aggressively; to Paul*) I think we've had about enough of your interference.

Paul (*indignantly*) *My* interference! Whose daughter is she—yours or mine?

Pam cries loudly

Charles Yours—*obviously!*

Paul (*advancing a step and thrusting his face into Charles*) Is that *meant* to be offensive, because . . .?

Pam cries even louder

Angela (*interrupting and jerking Charles away by the arm*) *Stop* it, you two! And Charles, you *must* be *just*. After all, she is his daughter, and taking an interest in her is not like telling you where to stand.

Charles (*huffily*) All right, then! Go on—*be* just—and see where it gets you. (*He throws himself into the easy chair and incidentally on to the bouquet and toast-rack. He winces at contact with the latter, turns, fishes them both out, looks vaguely for somewhere to put them and remains holding them in his lap*)

Throughout this row, Pam has stood looking from one to another and howling unrestrainedly. Mrs Mandrake has provided a more discreet background of sobs, sniffs, and gasps. Paul crosses to the desk

Mrs Mandrake (*moaningly*) If *only* you had let me . . .

Angela (*interrupting*) Oh, for heaven's sake leave off about her tonsils. (*She crosses to Pam*)

Pam sits on the stool

Pam—for the last time . . .

Pam (*interrupting*) *No!*

Angela (*indicating the despondent assembly*) You see what you've done already—and it's hardly *started* yet. (*She moves above the easy chair*)

Pam (*moving up stage to the piano; blubbering*) Anybody 'ud think I was en*joy*ing myself. It's no fun for *me*—calling it off. I've looked forward to it like *any*thing. (*She sinks on to the piano stool and slumps over the keyboard with her head in her arms*)

Angela (*crossing down C to the front of the chesterfield*) Well, the *next* time you want to get married, don't expect *me* to have anything to do with it. (*She flops fuming into the chesterfield*)

Mrs Coot enters R somewhat hesitantly. As she moves above the chesterfield and comes down C to get her bucket and then moves up to the piano for her mop the atmosphere of the room is borne in upon her and her habitual expression of defensive disapproval gives place to that of alarmed astonishment. She picks up her things, and retreats with them, casting startled glances at the silent and huddled forms about her. She exits R

Paul (*after slight pause*) What happens now?

Angela Don't ask me. I wash my hands of the whole business.

Millicent enters R

Millicent (*coming in as usual with a rush to* C; *in breathless triumph*) I'm ready.
Angela (*in a flat voice*) Are you, dear? That's nice.
Millicent (*looking from one to another*) What's the matter?

Silence. Nobody moves

(*In growing alarm*) Is anything wrong? (*She moves up to* L *of the piano*)
Angela (*rising in gloomy despair; addressing the world in general*) I simply don't know how to *tell* people things like this. (*She moves to* R)

Millicent stands looking bewildered

Joe is seen to hurry past the window from off L. *He is a large, single-minded young man with a simple philosophy and a patient nature, but possessing stormy potentialities as yet unplumbed. He can be driven too far. He wears the conventional morning coat, etc. He enters up* RC

Joe (*his head and shoulders appearing round the door; anxiously to Angela*) I say—are you sure this is all right?
Angela (*in a strangled voice*) Joe!
Joe I mean—isn't it supposed to be unlucky—me coming in like this?

Angela moves up R *to Joe with outstretched hand and draws him into the room. As she does so the first peals of the wedding-bells are heard*

Angela Come here! (*She leads him down* C)
Joe (*halting* C *and, with an expression of delight, holding up a finger*) Listen!
Angela (*moving down* R) Yes, dear! (*She sinks into the chesterfield*)

Pam chokes and bursts into renewed tears. Mrs Mandrake follows suit. Joe looks about him in dawning and horrified bewilderment. The wedding-bells peal out more joyously than ever

CURTAIN

ACT II

The same. After lunch the same day

Apart from a few remaining scraps of paper on the floor, the room is now reasonably tidy. Pam's suitcase still stands down C. Her prayer-book is on the piano. The door up RC is open

When the CURTAIN *rises Mrs Mandrake, dressed now in her workaday clothes, is engaged in thrusting a carpet-sweeper back and forth. She looks sadder than ever. The telephone bell begins to ring. With a long-suffering sigh Mrs Mandrake props the carpet-sweeper against the piano, goes to the desk and picks up the receiver*

Mrs Mandrake (*into the phone*) Yes? ... No, this is Mrs Mandrake. Mrs Dickson is out. ... Oh yes, Mrs Bedford! ... Yes, it *was* unfortunate this morning. We're all *very* upset. ... Yes, she was taken ill, poor darling. ... Well, I don't know really. She—er—she lost the use of her legs. ... Yes, and she couldn't—erm—couldn't see or breathe very well, and—er—I beg pardon? ... Oh yes, distinctly green. ... Well, we didn't have the doctor; we didn't think it was worth it. ... Oh, I'm sure it was nothing. We're only so sorry on account of all the trouble to which you were put to. ... Oh yes, the bells *were* nice—but it's not really the same thing if there's no wedding, is it? ... Yes, thank you so much, Mrs Bedford. ... Yes, I'll tell her. ... Good-bye! (*She replaces the receiver*)

Mrs Coot enters R. She wears a hat and overcoat

Mrs Coot (*remaining at the door R*) I'm orf.
Mrs Mandrake Very well, Mrs Coot.
Mrs Coot (*moving below the chesterfield*) Shan't be in 'sevenin'.
Mrs Mandrake (*slightly startled*) Oh?
Mrs Coot Or termorrer.
Mrs Mandrake (*dismayed*) No?
Mrs Coot No, I'm finished 'ere.
Mrs Mandrake Why, has ...?
Mrs Coot (*interrupting*) I don't like the way they *do* things.
Mrs Mandrake We're extremely sorry if you've been put out, Mrs Coot, but Miss Pam was taken ill.
Mrs Coot Ar—well, it's just as well if you ask me. Barmy ones like 'er 'aven't got no right to get married. They only pass it on.

Mrs Coot turns and exits R

Mrs Mandrake (*sighing wearily*) Oh *dear*, oh dear! (*Automatically she picks* *up one or two scraps of paper; then her eye is caught by Pam's suitcase. She approaches it and stands mournfully shaking her head at it)*

Pam enters up RC *from off* R. *She wears a simple frock. Her manner is very subdued. She sidles unobtrusively into the doorway, halts and leans against the doorpost, watching*

Mrs Mandrake lifts the suitcase and makes to move away with it

Pam *I'll* see to that, Mandy.

Mrs Mandrake (*starting slightly and replacing the suitcase*) Oh—very well, Miss Pam. (*She moves to* R, *taking out handkerchief and dabbing at her eyes, and halts at the door*) You wouldn't drink a nice, hot cup of tea, would you?

Pam (*smiling wanly*) No, thank you.

Mrs Mandrake You know what your dear grandmother used to say—there's nothing like hot tea with which to fortify oneself for the battle of life with.

Pam I know, dear, but ... (*She breaks off*)

Mrs Mandrake goes tragically out

Pam's eyes come round to the suitcase, and she moves slowly down to it. For a moment she, too, regards it with deep sadness; then, with a sob, she falls to her knees and encircles it with her arms, remaining thus with her head resting sideways upon it and emitting gentle, spasmodic gasps

Joe passes the window from off L *and enters up* RC. *He wears grey flannel slacks and a sports jacket. His manner is anxious and diffident. He halts up* L *of the chesterfield and regards Pam's backview for a moment with some surprise. Then he crosses to* R *above the chesterfield*

Joe (*moving below the chesterfield to Pam*) What's the matter?

Pam (*looking up; startled*) Oh, hullo, Joe!

Joe What you doing down there?

Pam Nothing much! —Just—holding my suitcase.

Joe (*perplexed*) What for?

Pam I—*felt* like it, that's all. (*She gets rather foolishly to her feet wiping an eye on the back of her hand*)

Joe (*vaguely*) Oh! (*He pauses uncomfortably; then falsely brisk*) Well, I just happened to be passing, so I thought I'd—sort of—pop in and ... (*He trails off*)

Pam (*politely*) I'm glad you did. (*She moves away to* LC)

There is a pause. Both are very ill-at-ease

(*Keeping her back to him, she blows her nose, then:*) Joe.

Joe Yes?

Pam Have you had any lunch?

Joe No.

Pam (*turning; concerned*) Oh Joe, why didn't you go with the others?

Joe Pam, you couldn't expect *me* to turn up at the ... (*He breaks off*)

Pam But it *was*n't a reception any more, dear, and the stuff was *there* and it had to be *paid* for. It might as well be *eaten*.

Joe Well, I hadn't much appetite, anyway.
Pam (*in a subdued tone*) No—I suppose not.

Pause

Joe (*accusingly*) You were crying, weren't you?
Pam (*with bent head*) A bit.
Joe Why?
Pam (*near to breaking down again*) I wanted so much to get married, Joe.
Joe (*perplexed*) But I thought it was you who—called it off.
Pam So it was.
Joe (*at a loss*) Well, then . . .!

Pam turns and looks at Joe; then she runs to him

Pam (*putting her arms round him*) Poor Joe! You do look so bewildered.
Joe (*standing rather stiffly*) Oh, I'm not bewildered, only—well, I happened
    to be passing and I thought I'd just look in and—find out what I'd done.
Pam (*uncomprehendingly*) What you'd done?
Joe Yes, well, I mean, you must be pretty wild about something to stand me
    up at the last minute like that.
Pam (*compassionately*) Oh my poor pet, *you* haven't done anything.
Joe Haven't I?
Pam Of *course* not. And *I'm* not wild.
Joe You're not?
Pam (*clinging to him*) No! (*She kisses him on the cheek*)
Joe (*throwing her off with sudden violence*) Then what the hell's it all about?
Pam (*peering at him critically*) Joe—are you angry?
Joe (*beginning to gesticulate*) Of *course* I'm angry.
Pam (*in a disappointed voice*) Joe!
Joe Well, how would you feel if you'd hired a morning suit and everything,
    and got a chap all the way down from Scotland to be your best man?
Pam (*with real contrition*) Joe, I'm so sorry. You don't *know* how sorry I
    am.
Joe (*stepping over the suitcase and crossing to* LC, *still waving his arms
    about*) And then to have to crawl home and change back into grey flannel
    trousers with the church bells still ringing! It makes you feel such a *fool*.
Pam Well, so long as it's only your vanity that's piqued, I don't mind so
    much. I was so terribly afraid you'd be hurt.
Joe (*moving* R *of the easy chair; violently*) I *am* hurt.
Pam You don't look it, Joe.
Joe (*resentfully*) What do you expect me to do—burst into tears? (*Giving
    way to self-pity*) If you'd *really* been taken ill I wouldn't have *min*ded.
    *No*body would have minded. But as it is, *e*verybody knows it's just a
    damn silly excuse and instead of being sorry for *you* they're sorry for *me*—
    and I don't *like* people being sorry for me. (*His voice breaks and he turns
    away to hide his emotion*)
Pam (*rushing at him full of concern*) Joe!

*She throws her arms round him from behind and dodges from side to side in an
effort to look into his face. Joe turns and re-turns his head to prevent her
doing so*

Joe, my sweet, my poppet!—Joe, darling, don't! *Please* don't!

Joe (*emotionally irritable*) Don't *what?*

Pam Don't cry, dear! You *must*n't cry! I can't *bear* it if you do that.

Joe (*angrily*) I'm *not* crying, you silly fool!

Pam (*still trying to look into his face*) Well, what *are* you doing?

Joe Nothing! (*Shaking himself free*) Go away and leave me alone! (*He moves to the fireplace*)

Pam, without resentment, but looking worried, goes to the chesterfield and sits

Pam If you're going to be hurt, I don't know *what* I'm going to do. It's quite complicated enough as it is.

Joe (*under control again*) What you're *going* to do! I should have thought you'd *done* it. (*His mood softens. He crosses to the chesterfield and sits* L *beside her*) Pam—don't you love me any more? Is that it?

Pam (*earnestly*) Oh no, Joe.

Joe You mean you don't, or that's not it?

Pam I *do* love you. I'm *sure* I do.

Joe (*plaintively*) Well, then—what *is* all this?

Pam hesitates, looking worried

(*Pathetically*) I only want to know *why*. It's not asking much.

Pam I doubt if I could ever make you understand. You see—I have every respect for your intelligence, Joe dear—but you haven't got what I should call a *subtle* mind.

Joe And that's what you need to appreciate a situation like this?

Pam Yes, in a way.

Joe I see. So the next time someone kicks me in the face with hobnail boots I shall know it's too subtle for me to understand.

Pam Don't be bitter, dear!

Joe (*controlling himself and continuing in a reasonable voice*) Look, Pam! Let's be objective. Here's a chap who's due to get married at twelve-thirty—see? He's got a pal to come all the way down from Scotland to . . .

Pam (*interrupting quite kindly*) Yes, *I* know.

Joe At twelve-twenty-five he's suddenly informed that he's not going to be married after all because, *A*, the bride's been reading the prayer-book and, *B*, her father doesn't seem such a bad chap after all. Well, I may be a bit dim, but it seems to me that you've got to be something more than subtle to sort that out.

Pam (*wretchedly*) I know it sounds odd when you put it like that.

Joe (*bitterly*) Odd! (*He folds his arms and sinks back gloomily*)

Pam Joe dear—don't let's quarrel. (*She takes his face in her two hands and kisses him*)

Joe (*forcibly removing her hands; irritably*) And please don't *do* that!

Pam (*dismayed*) Don't you want me to kiss you any more?

Joe I may be a bit old-fashioned, but to me there's something faintly indecent about giving a chap the chuck before lunch and getting gay with him immediately after.

Pam (*indignantly*) I'm *not* getting gay. And what on earth makes you think I've given you the chuck?

Joe Well, haven't you?

Pam *No!*

Joe (*sitting forward*) Are you trying to tell me we're still supposed to be engaged?

Pam Of *course!*

Joe To be married?

Pam *Yes*, Joe!

Joe (*sarcastically*) You mean it's only *this* particular wedding that's off ?

Pam Yes.

Joe Oh!

Pam Well—I hope so.

Joe (*deeply defeatist*) Pam, I don't think I could go through it all over again, really I don't—even if I *knew* it was going to lead to something.

Pam I wouldn't ask you to, dear.

Joe (*with a note of alarm*) You wouldn't?

Pam No. Our banns are read and everything, so I thought—next time, all we need do is just pop round to the vicar and . . . (*She breaks off*)

Joe (*turning to her, suddenly hopefully tender*) Oh, Pam! Do you mean that?

Pam If there *is* a next time.

Joe (*with a despairing gesture, rising*) I give up. (*He goes to the door up* RC *and stands staring gloomily out*)

Pam (*thoughtfully*) You see, Joe—I came to the conclusion this morning that we don't really know each other well enough to get married—not yet—not if you realize how *per*manent marriage is. I love you——

Joe turns his head to her

—as far as I know——

Joe turns his head away again

—and I *want* to marry you. But I *don't* want to make the mistake that Mummy made. (*She turns and looks at his backview*)

Joe makes no response

So, if you don't mind, I think I'd like to study you for a bit.

Joe looks at her

For one thing, I don't understand men very well. We haven't *got* many in our family.

Joe (*speaking over his shoulder*) I wonder you've got *any* if you all go on like this every time you get married.

Pam (*disregarding this*) And *you* should take the opportunity of studying *me*.

Joe (*turning and coming down to her behind the chesterfield*) Look; I don't *care* about your faults and weaknesses. I'm not even concerned with your *mother's* mistakes. (*Thumping the back of the chesterfield for emphasis*) *All I know is*—I *love you*.

Pam Well, that's very nice, but I doubt if it's quite the right attitude. What you should do is decide whether I'm *worthy* of your love.

Joe (*wandering away down* C; *darkly*) I've already decided about that.

Pam Then there are the various *a*spects of love to be considered.
Joe Such as?
Pam Well, the spiritual and the—physical, for instance.
Joe (*wearily*) I see.
Pam Incidentally I'm—grateful to you for not over-emphasizing the latter.
Joe Don't mention it! Why?
Pam Because that would only confuse the issue.
Joe (*sarcastically*) Oh, and we don't want to get the issue confused, do we?
Pam Still, I'm sure *that's* all right.
Joe What is?
Pam (*a little shyly*) The *phy*sical side, Joe.
Joe Oh well, that's something. (*He moves up stage and leans on the piano*)
Pam But the thing is—do we res*pect* and ad*mire* each other? Have we absolute *con*fidence in each other?
Joe (*emphatically*) Speaking for myself—*no!*
Pam (*startled*) Uh?
Joe (*coming down to her and leaning aggressively over the back of the chesterfield*) I neither admire *nor* respect you, and after this morning's performance I can think of *no*-one in whom I have less confidence.
Pam (*in a small voice*) Well, there you are, you see—you're already finding out things about me that you didn't know.
Joe (*violently*) But I *still* love you and I still want to *marry* you. (*He stumps up stage*)
Pam (*in a worried voice*) Oh Joe!
Joe (*halting*) Though, at the moment I doubt whether even the *phy*sical side's all right. (*Gloomily*) I'm going to get an apple.

He exits up RC *and goes off* R. *Pam rises and runs up stage in pursuit. At the same time Paul and Millicent, dressed as in Act I, are seen to pass the window from off* L. *They enter up* RC. *Paul carries a large cardboard soap-box and comes down* LC

Pam (*encountering them at door, halting*) Oh, hullo!
Millicent Hullo! (*She moves towards the piano*)

There is an air of embarrassed constraint between them

Pam (*after a pause*) Back again, then?
Paul (*dumping the box on the floor down* LC) Yes—yes—back again!

There is an awkward pause during which Millicent collapses on to the piano stool and fans herself with her hands. Paul moves up to L *of the piano and mops his brow*

Pam (*coming down to the back of the chesterfield; a little wistfully*) What was it like?
Millicent What?
Pam The reception. I mean, what *would* it have been like?
Millicent (*enthusiastically*) Oh, beautifully done—wasn't it, Mr Dickson?
Paul Excellently! The sandwiches were delicious.
Millicent And there was jelly and trifle and ice-cream and all *sorts* of things. *You* would have *loved* it.

Pam Anybody there?

Millicent Only the vicar. Everybody else went home—naturally.

Pam What did *he* think about it all?

Millicent The vicar? Well, there was a bit of a scene with him at first, but he's all right now, I think. Your mother gave him some tarts to take home.

They all laugh rather falsely. There is another pause during which they all stare at the soap-box

Pam (*indicating the soap-box*) What *is* that?

Paul Sausage-rolls. I think.

They laugh again. Slight pause

Millicent (*rising*) I'll take 'em out, shall I? (*She comes down* LC)

Pam Will you? Thanks!

Millicent lifts the soap-box with an effort and crosses towards the door R. *Paul crosses to open the door for her*

Millicent (*giving Paul a flashing smile as she passes*) Thank you!

Millicent exits R

Pam notices the carpet-sweeper, takes hold of it and begins to use it up C. *Paul moves in to the* R *end of the chesterfield, watching her*

Pam (*after a slight pause; a little self-consciously*) I suppose you think I'm a pretty extraordinary person?

Paul (*with a tolerant half-smile*) I knew your mother, Pam.

Pam Was she so like me?

Paul So like you that—my heart bleeds for that young man. (*He indicates the departed Joe*)

Pam (*stopping sweeping; with a note of surprise*) *She* didn't start up anything like this, did she?

Paul If she didn't, it was only because she didn't think of it.

Pam Ah! That's where she went wrong. (*She continues sweeping*)

Paul (*sitting on the chesterfield; faintly aggrieved*) I don't know why it should be taken for granted that it was necessarily *Angela* who went wrong in marrying *me*. And, in any case, Pam—may I say that I think you're making certain basic errors in your whole approach to matrimony?

Pam (*interested*) Oh? What?

Paul Well, mainly in letting other people's experiences influence you.

Pam (*stopping sweeping and standing* C, *looking worried*) I know it sounds mad. But—when you came in this morning—you seemed so nice—and I remembered how sweet you'd been in Switzerland—and I thought, well, if he's a rotter it doesn't show—and that's disturbing—and if he's *not* a rotter, why can't two thoroughly well-meaning people like him and Mummy get on?—and that's more disturbing still. So, what with one thing and another ... (*She breaks off and continues sweeping down* L)

Paul You know—I think you're making too much of a bogey of that.

Pam (*stopping sweeping*) You mean—of Mummy and you?

Paul Yes.

Pam But *surely* there's *noth*ing worse?

Paul I wouldn't have missed it, Pam.

Pam (*staring at him incredulously*) You *would*n't have *missed* it?

Paul No—I've much to be grateful to Angela for. A span of vigorous living! Some good memories and—something sort of—precious that survives.

Pam (*gazing at him tenderly and emitting the feminine exclamation meaning "how sweet"*) Ahoouh!

Paul I'll tell you something, shall I?

Pam Do—please! (*She leans the sweeper against the mantelpiece and stands at the fireplace*)

Paul When I came in this morning, I said I'd come because of the wedding. That was true, of course,—but only half true—because it was an excuse. I *really* wanted to see Angela.

Pam You mean—you mean you still . . .?

Paul (*hurriedly*) Good heavens, no! You mustn't think that. I just felt I wanted to *see* her, that's all—see what she looked like after all this time. Hear her voice! *You* know!

Pam (*enchanted*) Well, *I* think you're a *lamb*. (*Indignantly*) And after the way she's *trea*ted you . . .!

Angela enters L through the porch. She is dressed as in Act I and carries a large and bulging paper carrier-bag

Paul (*urgently*) Look here! You mustn't think that I'm trying to put any blame on Angela, because . . . (*He breaks off and rises as he sees her*)

Angela (*ignoring Paul, coming straight down to Pam with a look of concern*) Darling—how do you feel now?

Pam (*faintly irritable*) *I'm* all right, Mummy.

Angela Oh, of *course* you are. I've told so many lies about your health during the last hour or so, that I . . . (*She breaks off, crosses up stage and deposits the carrier on the piano stool*)

Charles enters L through the porch. He is dressed as in Act I and looks hot and irritable. He is wearing his top-hat and carries before him, as on a tray, the wedding-cake

(*To Charles*) Put it down somewhere, dear. (*She moves to the back of the easy chair*)

Charles looks vaguely and vainly round for somewhere to put the cake, crosses to the back of the chesterfield, and remains holding it

(*To Paul; coldly*) May I ask what it is that you don't blame me for?

Paul (*below the chesterfield, R end; startled and embarrassed*) What? Well, I . . .

Pam (*intervening*) Simply for not being able to live with him, Mummy, that's all.

Angela (*sarcastically*) Oh, is *that* all?

Pam He didn't say anything in the *least* disloyal and there's *noth*ing to get excited about.

Angela (*crossing below the chesterfield*) Oh, but I think it's *most* exciting to know that I'm not to blame for being unable to live with him. We've all worried *so* much about that—haven't we, Charles?

Charles (*beginning uncomfortably*) Look here, Angela . . .!

Angela (*interrupting; to Paul*) Were you thinking of leaving soon?

Charles moves up C *to the piano*

Paul (*awkwardly*) I thought I'd just say good-bye to young whatsisname (*he indicates the garden*)—and then . . . (*He breaks off*)

Angela (*crossing to the door* R) A very good idea! (*She opens the door and calls*) Mandy!

Paul hesitates uncertainly, then moves up R *to the door up* RC

Pam You'll come back and say good-bye to *me*, won't you?

Paul (*at the door*) Of course.

Charles (*to Paul*) I say . . .!

Paul Yes?

Charles Would you mind taking my hat off?

Paul removes Charles' top-hat, plonks it on the piano and goes out up RC *and off* R. *He shuts the door*

Pam (*at once remonstrating*) Mummy—what*ever* his faults, you *can't* get away from the fact that you *have* been his wife and—and borne his children and everything.

Angela What *do* you mean?

Pam Well, surely it must mean *some*thing to you. You *can't* send him off like this.

Angela (*crossing to* LC) In any case I have *not* borne his children. I've borne him *one* child, and I'm inclined to think even that's a pity. (*She is* R *of the easy chair*)

Charles (*coming a few steps down* C; *uncomfortably*) Haven't you two got any reticence at all?

Pam (*smugly*) Well, I'm sure *I* should never treat an ex-husband like that.

Angela Let's hope you'll never have one.

Charles She won't at this rate.

Angela (*to Pam*) What do you expect me to do—(*sarcastically*) invite him to stay for a week or so?

Pam (*moving towards Angela*) As a matter of fact, that's exactly what I was going to suggest. (*She kneels in the easy chair*)

Angela (*astonished*) You were *what*?

Charles What on earth for?

Pam I'm his *daugh*ter. I've got a *right* to know him.

Angela But, darling, we couldn't have him *here*. Apart from anything else, it wouldn't be—respectable.

Pam Why not? You've got Mandy if you want a chaperone. Nobody 'ud mind if *Charles* stayed.

Angela That's en*tirely* different. Charles has never . . . I haven't been . . .

Charles (*intervening*) Different thing altogether!

Angela Yes.

Mrs Mandrake enters R

Pam sighs and moves to the fireplace

Mrs Mandrake Did you call?
Angela (*crossing below the chesterfield to* R) Yes, Mandy. There are some more things in that carrier. (*She indicates the bag on the piano stool*)— And, er—(*she notices Charles*) Charles dear, *do* put that down!

Mrs Mandrake goes to the piano stool for the carrier

Charles (*plaintively*) I don't know where to *put* the damn thing.
Angela (*going to him*) Well, give it to me! Don't be so helpless! (*She takes the cake from Charles, moves below the chesterfield, looks vaguely round and remains holding it*)

Charles crosses to R *above the chesterfield*

Mrs Mandrake (*coming down* C) What *are* we to do with it, Miss Angela? (*She moves below the chesterfield*)
Angela (*hopelessly*) I don't know, Mandy. You can't sit down and eat a thing like that in cold blood.
Charles Couldn't you make a trifle out of it?
Angela (*dismissing the suggestion with mild scorn*) Charles! Pam, dear— what do you want us to do with it?

Charles move behind the chesterfield

Pam Won't it keep?
Mrs Mandrake Well, you know what the present-day flour is.
Pam I know, but—there's no point about getting another if it *will* keep.
Angela (*uneasily*) Getting another?
Charles Are you suggesting that we should have it for *our* wedding? (*He crosses to* LC *towards Pam*)
Pam No, of course not! My next!

Mrs Mandrake emits a gasping noise indicating mingled exasperation and dread and puts the carrier on the chesterfield

Angela Pam—are you proposing to begin this extraordinary performance all over again?
Pam No, but you must have a cake for *any* sort of marriage.
Charles So you still regard yourself as engaged to be married?
Pam Certainly!
Angela (*wearily*) I see. So long as we know! (*She hands the cake to Mrs Mandrake*) Only, you *may* find, my dear, that the cake keeps better than Joseph.

She moves to the door R *and opens it for Mrs Mandrake. Charles sits rather wearily in the easy chair*

Mrs Mandrake And then there's the presents.
Angela Yes. (*To Pam*) What are you going to do about *them*? (*She comes below the chesterfield*)
Pam (*a shade impatiently*) Oh, *I* don't know, Mummy. They can go in the cupboard under the stairs, can't they?
Angela But we can't *keep* them, dear.

Pam Why not? I'm only supposed to be ill.

Angela But that's false pretences.

Pam Well, anyway, till we know what's happening. You can't expect people to keep on sending them back and forth, can you?

Angela No, I suppose not.

Mrs Mandrake (*crossing to the door* R; *dismally*) In any case—they've got so confused now that I doubt whether we should know to whom to send them to.

Mrs Mandrake exits R

Angela sinks into the chesterfield. Pam sighs and sits in the armchair down L. *Angela sighs. They both look extremely dispirited. Charles glances from one to the other then rises briskly*

Charles Come on, now! We don't want to get gloomy. What's the next thing?

Angela (*wearily*) *I* don't know, Charles. (*She looks dimly round the room*) You might take Pam's suitcase up for her.

Charles Right! (*He steps forward towards the case with alacrity*)

Pam (*rising and moving swiftly to the suitcase, intercepting Charles*) *I'*ll do it. (*With a faint, polite smile*) Thank you, Charles! (*She lifts the suitcase*) And, Mummy—please—I don't want it touched.

Charles moves behind the chesterfield

Angela (*in some surprise*) You're going to unpack it, aren't you?

Pam (*backing across to* R *with the suitcase suspended in both hands before her*) No, I—I suppose it's silly and sentimental of me, but I've got a sort of a superstitious feeling that if I don't keep it—just as it is—until I need it—something might go wrong.

Pam exits R

Angela (*turning her eyes to heaven as if for support*) She's got a feeling—that something *might* go wrong.

Charles (*coming round the* R *end of the chesterfield*) Look here, old girl ...

Angela (*a little wearily*) Charles dear—*must* you use that expression? In *any* case it's a contradiction of terms *nei*ther of which applies to me.

Charles (*crossing down stage to* LC) Sorry—I forgot. (*Beginning to walk thoughtfully about*) But listen, I've been thinking. This may sound strange to you, but I think it might be a good idea if you *did* ask this feller to stay for a bit.

Angela (*surprised*) *Paul?*

Charles Yes.

Angela *Stay?*

Charles Yes.

Angela What on *earth* for?

Charles Well, it's pretty evident that Pam's taken quite a fancy to him.

Angela I can't take him into my house simply because Pam happens to have taken a fancy to him, Charles.

Charles (*moving behind the chesterfield*) What I mean is—if you send him off like this—with a flea in his ear—you'll have her taking his side if you're not careful.

Angela Why?

Charles (*coming down* R *of the chesterfield*) Because you'll be making a martyr of him.

Angela (*alarmed*) Shall I?

Charles Certainly you will. That's simple psychology. (*He sits on the chesterfield*) Before you know it, *he*'ll become the hero of the piece and you and I'll be the—er, the—er . . .

Angela (*quite horrified*) Charles!

Charles (*gravely*) It's the sort of thing, old g—— my dear, that might turn a united family into anything but.

Angela So you thought . . .?

Charles I thought the simple remedy would be to let him stay for a bit and discredit himself.

Angela How would he be likely to do that?

Charles Well, I don't know. But if the chap's a bit of a cad, it's bound to come out sooner or later.

Angela (*a little sharply*) Who said he was a cad?

Charles (*rather taken aback*) Well—isn't he?

Angela Charles—you should know me well enough to know that I do *not* marry cads. In many ways Paul is a very charming man—and if he has a weakness, it's not the kind that "comes out".

Charles (*hopefully*) Doesn't he drink?

Angela He didn't when *I* knew him.

Charles (*optimistically*) He may have taken to it since. You never know.

Angela Nonsense, Charles!

Charles (*with a slightly huffy shrug*) Oh, very well!

Angela But I do think there might be something in what you say about giving Pam a chance to realize that—that at least he's no martyr.

Charles Exactly! And if, in the process, he *should* happen to slip up in some way, it might help to straighten out this idiotic marriage complex of hers too.

At this Angela cups her chin in her hand and begins to frown in laboured thought

And remember, my dear—if I *should* get sent abroad, and Pam's not fixed up, it may be awkward for *us*.

Angela Charles—can you explain to me *why* it is that Paul's behaviour should have anything to do with Pam marrying Joe? I *did* know at one time this morning, but somehow it seems to have escaped me.

Charles Well—it's perfectly simple. What with reading the marriage ceremony and so on, she's got it into her head that—er—that you wouldn't have married him if—er . . . that people oughtn't to get married unless—erm . . . Now, let me see . . .! (*He lapses into confused thought*)

The arguing voices of Millicent and Joe are heard from the garden

Joe		
	(*off; together*)	(*trying to get a word in*) All I know is . . . Look! All I . . .
Millicent		Men don't understand these things. You must try and see the woman's point of view.

Millicent and Joe enter up RC *from off* R. *Millicent moves to the piano*

Joe (*gesticulating with a half-eaten apple*) I know, but what I don't understand is what the hell all this has got to do with . . . (*He breaks off as he sees the others*) Oh!

Angela (*rising*) Oh, hullo, Joe! Did you see Paul?

Joe (*crossing to the easy chair*) Who?

Angela Paul. My—er—Pam's father.

Joe No, I didn't see him. Why?

Angela (*moving up to Joe*) He was looking for you, I think.

Joe What for?

Angela Just to say good-bye.

Joe (*morosely*) Good! (*He sits on the* R *arm of the easy chair, then recollects himself*) Oh, sorry, I . . .

Angela Never mind, dear! I know just how you feel. (*She stoops and kisses him*) Come along, Charles! (*She crosses to* R *above the chesterfield*)

Charles drags himself up

(*As she moves to the door* R) Bring the buns out for me, will you? (*She indicates the carrier on the chesterfield*)

With slightly less alacrity than usual, Charles picks up the carrier and follows

Angela (*pausing at the door* R; *thoughtfully*) Why, do you suppose, did Mr Atkins tell me in that rather pointed way that he was going to have his telephone cut off?

Charles (*going out*) I can't imagine.

Charles and Angela exit R

Joe (*at once, rising*) What *I* don't understand . . .

Millicent (*interrupting*) You can't be ex*pect*ed to understand, Joe. This is a *wo*man's thing.

Joe (*ironically*) Oh, I see!

Millicent It's all a matter of her father *not* looking what he *is*.

Joe (*uncomprehendingly*) Uh?

Millicent She *knows* what sort of a life he leads—and yet he seems nice—*very* nice, in fact.

Joe But . . .

Millicent (*interrupting*) *With* the result that she's got doubtful about *you*.

Joe Because *I'm* nice?

Millicent Yes—in a way.

Joe What do I do then—be nasty?

Millicent No, but . . . (*She breaks off, struck by a thought, moves quickly to the door up* RC *and closes it*) Joe—if only we could show *him* up in his true colours! (*She comes down* C *and sits on the* L *arm of the chesterfield*)

Joe Oh, for heaven's sake! (*He moves away, down* L)

Millicent (*warming to her idea; rising and following him*) No, listen, Joe! I'd do *any*thing for you and Pam—you *know* that. Would you call me attractive?

Joe (*a little startled*) Eh?

Millicent No—really!

Joe (*warily*) Well—it's a matter of taste.

Millicent What I mean is—do you think I've got what it takes to make a man—well—forget himself?

Joe Am I to understand that you're throwing yourself to me as a sop?

Millicent (*indignantly*) No, you are not! I don't mean a stupid, inhibited lout like you. I mean a seasoned man-of-the-world like Mr Dickson.

Joe (*sitting on the stool at the desk*) Should I know what the hell you're talking about or is this *another* woman's thing?

Millicent (*stiffly*) What I'm suggesting—for *your* sake—is that *I* should *encourage* Mr Dickson to show his less attractive side.

Joe (*suffering deeply*) Milly, look! You're a good kid, but *don't* stand there talking like a dramatic art student, *please*! I've got quite enough on my mind.

Millicent But, Joe . . .

Joe (*interrupting*) He's going, anyway.

Millicent He may stay to tea.

Joe I doubt if you'd get much done between now and teatime.

Paul enters up RC *from off* R

Here you are! Have a go! (*He grins, takes a bite out of his apple, rises and moves to the fireplace*)

Paul (*to Joe*) Oh, *there* you are! (*He crosses to* C)

Angela enters R

Angela (*to Paul; cordially*) Ah, *there* you are!

Paul (*thinking she must be addressing someone behind him, looks over his shoulder*) Who, me?

Angela (*advancing to Paul*) Yes, I was afraid you might have left. Paul, dear, I don't know *why* I didn't think of it before. It was extraordinarily stupid of me. But *must* you go back this evening?

Paul (*astounded*) What?

Angela (*very affably*) I mean—you've come all this way for the wedding and there hasn't been one and it *does* seem rather a pity not to stay and see something of Pam now that you're here.

Paul (*bewildered*) Well—yes, I . . .

Millicent (*moving in to Paul's* L; *enthusiastically*) Oh do, Mr Dickson!

Angela (*moving in to Paul's* R) It *would* be so nice if you could.

Paul (*uncertainly*) Well—I *have* got a bag at the *Station Hotel*.

Millicent Good!

Joe, at the fireplace, looks anything but pleased

Angela (*with satisfaction*) Then *that's* settled. (*She bustles up to* L *of the piano*) Millicent, dear, help me get some of these things under the stairs. (*She begins collecting presents*)

Millicent Yes, rather! (*She moves up to* R *of the piano*)

Paul wanders to the chesterfield, sits and lapses into puzzled thought

Joe (*moving up to the door* L; *awkwardly*) Well—I think I'll be getting along, Mrs Dickson.

Angela (*kindly*) Come in tonight, dear, if you haven't anything better to do. We're always glad to see you.

Joe (*apparently considering*) No, I don't think I've got anything better to do tonight.

Angela (*recollecting*) Oh no, of course—you wouldn't have, would you?

Joe exits L. *Millicent crosses to the door* R *with an armful of toast-racks etc. Charles enters* R. *He holds the door as Millicent passes through and exits*

Charles sees Angela stacking herself with presents and moves down R, *leaving the door open for her*

Paul (*rising*) Well, perhaps I'd better pop down and get my bag, then.

Angela Yes, do! (*To Charles*) Paul's staying for a week or so, dear.

Charles (*at the buffet; with every evidence of pleased surprise*) Oh, how very nice, my dear fellow! I'm delighted. Well—er—we'll try and fix a game of golf, eh?

Paul (*also pleased as well as surprised*) Yes—rather!

Angela (*coming down* C *and crossing below the chesterfield to the door* R *with her load*) Well—I'll leave you two to find out if you have anything else in common.

Charles We *should* have—eh? (*He begins to laugh, but catching Angela's unamused eye, turns it into a throat clearance and takes a bottle from the buffet*) Well, now—what about a quick one?

Angela halts and watches

Paul Not for me, thanks.

Charles (*a bit let down*) No?

Paul Bit early for me.

Charles (*with a hint of disappointment*) Oh!

Angela (*to Charles; cryptically*) You see?

Angela exits R *looking rather smug*

Charles Well, *I'm* going to. (*He takes a glass*) I've had a heavy day. Sure you won't?

Paul (*weakening*) All right, then! Just a spot—to be matey! (*He perches on the* R *arm of the chesterfield*)

Charles (*hopeful again*) Whisky?

Paul Thanks!

Charles pours whisky very liberally

Whoa! Steady!

Charles (*handing the glass to Paul and taking out the siphon*) You know—if I were Angela, I should be just a little bit (*he squirts a tiny drop of soda into Paul's glass*)—worried about this girl.

Paul Who—Pam?

Charles Yes. (*He begins mixing his own drink*)

Paul Good heavens! Why?

Charles Well—I don't know—but there seems to me to be something a bit unbalanced about this set-out of hers.

Paul Oh nonsense, my dear fellow! Angela was just like that.

Charles *Angela?*
Paul Yes.
Charles Like—like *this*? (*He indicates the situation*)
Paul Certainly. She still is really.
Charles Well, I—I can't say I've come across it. (*He crosses below the chesterfield towards* C)
Paul (*confidently*) You will. Cheerio! (*He drinks*)
Charles (*a little half-heartedly*) Cheerio! (*He drinks*)
Paul You see—I know her better than you do. (*Delicately*) When you—er—when you've actually been . . . Well, it's only natural.
Charles (*uncomfortably*) Oh, of course.
Paul I knew Angela's mother, too. She was just the same. They all are. Charming and mad. And yet you'll find there's usually an element of sound common-sense behind these apparent lunacies of theirs.
Charles There doesn't seem to be much common-sense about this thing of Pam's.
Paul I don't know. It's not *really* so daft, when you analyse it. After all—the wedding ceremony *is* a bit of a pill, and there's no doubt that people *don't* give enough thought to it.
Charles (*uneasily*) You don't think so? (*He moves towards Paul*)
Paul I'm sure of it. Consider the words "Till death do us part". "Till *death*"! It's a solemn thought, you know.
Charles (*with a trace of anxiety*) It is, rather, isn't it?
Paul (*rising*) So I shouldn't worry too much about *Pam*, if I were you.
Charles (*manifestly not worrying about Pam*) You wouldn't?
Paul No. Well! (*He drains his glass and puts it on the buffet*) See you later! (*He walks straight across to the doors* L *and throws a single appraising glance at Charles*)

Paul exits through the porch

Charles, looking faintly disturbed, remains staring after him. He drains his glass absently, sets it down and stands for a moment in thought. Then he goes rapidly to the piano, picks up the prayer-book, returns with it to the easy chair where, after a furtive glance left and right, he settles himself and opens the book

CURTAIN

SCENE 2

The same. After supper that evening

The pink, reflected light of sunset is rapidly fading

The CURTAIN *rises on an empty stage. The radio, however, has been left on, and from it issues a dull and unctuous voice*

Radio Voice . . . history of the English Parliament is, in a sense, that of the struggles between the king and the people. After that date it became the history of the struggle for electoral reform, and of the evolution of the doctrine of ministerial responsibility together with the development of the party system . . .

Joe passes the window from off L *and enters up* RC. *He is dressed as in the previous scene, but now wears, in addition, a muffler. He is the picture of gloom as he looks dully round the empty room. He removes the muffler and puts it on the piano, where the prayer-book is lying. He double-takes this, picks it up, looks at it, sighs and puts it down again. For a moment, he stands aimlessly, then crosses to the door* R *and listens. He sighs again, wanders down to the chesterfield, picks up "Woman and Home", glances at it and drops it back again. Meanwhile the radio continues*

The outstanding landmarks of the pre-revolutionary period are the resistance of the king and the people in alliance, to the tyranny of the feudal barons; and later the alliance of the barons and people against the encroachments of the royal prerogative, the admission to Parliament of the medieval burgesses ostensibly to be consulted on questions of taxation—the beginning of the development of popular representation— the alternating concentration of power, first in the hands of the monarchs and then in the commoners, between the end of the thirteenth century, and the close of the Tudor period . . .

Joe (*striding to the radio; irritably*) Oh—shut up! (*He switches off the radio*)

Angela enters R. *She wears an afternoon dress*

Angela (*crossing to the desk*) Oh, hullo, Joe! Can't you find anyone, dear?
Joe No, I . . .
Angela (*interrupting*) I'm so sorry. But we're all at sixes and sevens tonight. We've had *such* an upset. (*She begins searching through papers on the desk*)
Joe (*quite indignantly*) I know we have. I was mixed up in it. (*He crosses to* R *of the easy chair*)
Angela I don't mean *yours*, dear. Yours was this morning. This is another one.
Joe (*apprehensively*) Oh Lord! What's she done now?
Angela Oh, it's not Pam this time. It's Charles.
Joe Don't tell me *his* father's turned up.
Angela No, dear, he's been posted to Peru.
Joe (*unimpressed*) Oh!
Angela He had a message from the Foreign Office this evening and he's only got till the fourteenth to get ready and that means we shall have to be *married* within about a week—by special licence.
Joe (*trying to take a polite interest*) Oh—are *you* going?
Angela Of *course* I'm going. I *adore* the idea of Peru. Wouldn't *you*—if you were going to be married?
Joe (*gloomily*) I shouldn't care much where it was. (*He sits on the* R *arm of the easy chair*)
Angela (*stopping her rummaging and regarding Joe with compassion*) Poor Joe! I was forgetting. This was to have been your wedding night, wasn't it?

Joe shuffles and smirks foolishly

That's why I'm so sorry *this* had to happen. I was hoping to arrange a jolly evening with round games for you. (*She recommences her searching*)

Joe (*mumbling*) That's all right. (*In sudden alarm*) I say—what about Pam?

Angela (*a cloud passing over her face*) Pam, I regret to say, is being thoroughly obstructive. She thinks I'm blinded by Peru and rushing into it headlong.

Joe Yes, but . . .

Angela (*interrupting*) She thinks I know next to nothing about Charles—if you ever heard such nonsense—and that if I can't submit him to a long course of exhaustive investigation, I oughtn't to marry him at all.

Joe No, but, I mean, *she's* not going to Peru, is she?

Angela No. She's going to stay here with Mandy. *Noth*ing would make her leave *you*, Joe.

Joe (*his face lighting up*) Did she say that?

Angela Yes—well—not in the middle of her research, anyway.

Joe (*his face falling again*) Oh! (*He sinks into the easy chair*)

Angela (*suddenly straightening up with a puzzled look*) What am I *looking* for? (*She ponders*) Oh yes—coupons! (*She recommences searching*) How on *earth* I'm going to get everything ready by tomorrow week, I *don't* know.

Joe I say—would you mind telling me something?

Angela Certainly, dear!

Joe (*hesitating slightly*) In what way have I failed?

Angela You mean with Pam?

Joe Yes.

Angela Oh, I wouldn't say that you've *failed*, dear—not com*plete*ly.

Joe Well, I haven't exactly got everything buttoned up, have I?

Angela Pam has her own way of doing things.

Joe Yes, I gathered that. But there must be something wrong with me, too.

Angela (*straightening up and giving him her full attention*) Joe—if I may say so—I think you should be a little more *master*ful with her. (*She moves down* L)

Joe Who, me? Masterful?

Angela Yes—com*pell*ing!

Joe With *Pam*?

Angela Certainly! Pam is the type of girl who should be taken by storm. She can't be wooed. I think you're making the mistake of trying to *woo* her.

Joe (*quite startled*) Am I?

Angela That's my impression, dear.

Joe Anyway, I thought I'd got all that part *done*.

Angela (*sympathetically*) I know, dear, and it's too bad—but what she really needs is a *whirl*wind courtship—something that doesn't give her a chance to *think*, because once she starts thinking, it's fatal. (*As she crosses to* C) I know because she's so like me.

Joe (*wearily*) Oh Lord!

Angela (*startled*) Uh?

Joe (*hurriedly*) No, no, I don't mean that. I mean I—well, I'm just not a whirlwind sort of chap. (*Sprawled gloomily, he looks anything but*)

Angela (*looking at him doubtfully*) I know you're not, dear. But I do think an effort might be worth your while. If you could show a little more—

well, a little more *fire*! Not for long. There's no need to keep it up. Just enough to see her over this crisis, that's all.

Joe (*worried*) But I shouldn't know how to set about taking a girl by assault—I mean storm.

Angela Well, anyway ... (*She breaks off, goes again to the desk and recommences searching*)

Mrs Mandrake enters R. *She is dressed as in the previous scene*

Mrs Mandrake (*putting her head round the door*) Shall I ask Sir Charles to get your trunks out of the loft, Miss Angela?

Angela Well, let the poor man finish washing up, Mandy.

Joe (*making to rise*) I'll do it.

Angela No, dear, you've had a very trying day.

Joe subsides again on to the R *arm of the easy chair and lapses into worried abstraction*

(*To Mrs Mandrake*) Where's Mr Paul?

Mrs Mandrake (*acidly*) Wasting his time with Miss Millicent outside. At least—I *hope* he's wasting his time. (*She crosses towards* C *below the chesterfield*) What are you looking for?

Angela Coupons!

Mrs Mandrake (*a little guiltily*) Oh, I forgot to tell you. They were in your room. (*She crosses to Angela with the coupon book in her hand*)

Angela (*in mild exasperation*) Oh Mandy! (*She moves down to meet Mrs Mandrake and takes the coupon book*)

Pam enters R. *She is dressed as in the previous scene and carries an enormous book which she reads as she walks. She throws a thin smile at Joe and crosses to the* L *end of the chesterfield, where she sits on the arm and continues reading. Joe smiles sourly in return, rises, retires up* L *to the small upright chair, sits and remains hunched up, sullenly staring at Pam*

(*She looks in the coupon book*) Heavens! There aren't many, are there?

Mrs Mandrake Well, you used them up on Miss Pam, didn't you?

Angela (*considering*) Now, what shall I *need*?

Mrs Mandrake That depends on the climate to which you are going to.

Pam A raincoat and an umbrella, anyway.

Angela What on earth for? Peru's tropical.

Pam It says here—"From June to September mists establish themselves for weeks together—accompanied by drizzling rain."

Angela What have you got there?

Pam (*holding up the book*) Encyclopaedia! Peru! You'll want some good thick walking shoes, too. (*Reading*) "Roads and bridges are few and bad, and mule traffic is still the chief means of ..."

Angela (*crossing to Pam; interrupting determinedly*) Now listen, Pam! Nobody can prevent you from complicating your own life by this habit of looking things up at the last minute—but I will *not* have *my* affairs disrupted by the Encyclopaedia Britannica.

Pam (*suddenly solicitous*) Mummy—if I thought you *really* knew what you

were doing—if I thought you were quite, *quite* happy about it your*self*—
I'd do *any*thing to ... (*She breaks off*)

Charles enters R. *He is dressed as in the previous scene and is wiping his
hands on a tea-cloth. He looks tired and rather dishevelled. He has lost his
bounce*

Angela Charles—what *is* the climate in Peru?

Charles (*doubtfully*) Well ...

Pam (*interrupting; reading*) "On the whole the climate is enervating, but
..."

Angela (*interrupting*) I was asking Charles. (*She crosses below the
chesterfield to Charles*)

Charles (*with a note of warning*) I'm afraid it's nothing to brag about where
we shall be, my dear. I don't want you to get any false ideas, you know.
(*He realizes that he has the tea-cloth, seems undecided what to do with it
and sticks a corner of it in his trouser pocket, so that it hangs down his leg*)

Pam (*studying the book; with false satisfaction*) There's not much yellow-
fever or plague, though. That's nice!

Charles No, malaria's the chief problem. (*He crosses to* C)

Pam Oh yes, that's all *over* the shop. *And*, of course, you've got to look out
for *snakes*. Still—there are several good harbours—and extensive coal
deposits. You can't have everything. (*She grins mischievously*)

Angela I don't care *what* you say, Pam. I'm *going* to Peru and I'm going to
en*joy* Peru.

Charles (*wearily*) Look—I think I'll push along now, if you don't mind. I've
got an awful lot to see to at home.

Angela (*moving towards the door* R) All right, dear, but just give me a hand
with a couple of trunks first, will you?

Charles, endeavouring to suppress a sigh, crosses up stage to the door R *and
exits*

(*At the door; to Pam*) We shall be able to use your wedding-cake too.

Angela exits R

Mrs Mandrake (*crossing to the door* R) Oh, *why* did it have to be Peru? It
was bad enough when I thought she was going to marry that man who
lived at Notting Hill Gate.

Mrs Mandrake exits R

*Pam continues reading. For some moments Joe sits moodily staring at her,
then he rises, braces himself and walks purposefully down towards her. Pam
looks up enquiringly. Joe checks himself, hesitates, loses heart, wanders up to
radio and switches it on. Pam goes on reading*

Radio Voice ... by calling them "Parliaments" instead of the Magnum
Concilium ...

Joe Oh, my God! (*He switches the radio off. He stands for a moment staring
at the back of Pam's head, then a look of determination comes over him. He
strides purposefully down to the chesterfield, leans over the back of it, seizes*

*Pam, kisses her with considerable violence and, after an undignified struggle
to regain his balance, straightens up again, looking defiant)*
Pam *(in some surprise)* What's the matter with *you?*
Joe *(resentfully)* Nothing's the matter with me.
Pam Well—all right—don't get huffy!

*Joe seats himself morosely on the back of the chesterfield with his back to her.
There is a pause*

> *(She lays her book aside; with a change of tone)* I'm so worried about
> Mummy, Joe. I can't bear to think of her undertaking to cherish Charles
> indefinitely. I'm sure she won't be able to keep it up for long. And then—
> now that my father's come back ... Do you know, Joe—he's evidently
> been thinking about her, off and on, for sixteen years? *(She looks up at his
> unresponsive backview)* Are you paying the slightest attention to me?
Joe *(unequivocally)* No!

Pam rises, walks round to Joe and peers anxiously into his face

Pam Are you all right?

*For answer, Joe gets deliberately off the chesterfield, grabs her in a bear-like
embrace, kisses her and shoves her roughly off again*

> *(Startled and a little shaken—panting)* What *is* this? *(She is below the easy
> chair)*
Joe *(at* C; *indignantly)* What do you *mean,* what is it?
Pam Why do you suddenly start doing that—like that?
Joe I've got to start some time, haven't I?
Pam *(frankly perplexed)* I don't see why.
Joe Oh, you don't! Well, the sooner you find out, the better.

*He grabs her by the wrist, strides with her trailing behind him to the easy chair,
throws himself into it and pulls her roughly on to his lap*

Pam *(struggling to get up)* Joe, what's the *matter* with you? *Stop* it!
Joe *(holding her)* Sit down and keep quiet!
Pam *(struggling)* Don't be such an idiot, Joe! Someone might come *in.*
Joe What the hell does it matter if they *do* come in? We're going to be
    married, aren't we?
Pam We're not married *yet,* though. *(Struggling violently)* Let me *go!*
Joe *(forcing her head down on to his chest)* Sit still and stop being coy!
Pam *(immediately bobbing up again; angrily)* Joe, if you don't stop this
    nonsense, I'll *smack* your *face.*
Joe *(suddenly roaring at her) Shut up!*

*Pam, startled into stillness, stops struggling and sits looking at him with wide
eyes*

Pam *(in a shocked but small and scared voice)* Joe!
Joe *(drawing her head down again, though more gently)* Now then! Keep still
    and give me a chance to be a bit demonstrative.
Pam *(wonderingly)* Is that what you're doing?
Joe What do you *think* I'm doing?

Pam (*making one more half-hearted attempt to sit up*) But Joe—there's no
need to be aggressive ab——
Joe (*interrupting*) Quiet!

Pam, of her own accord, subsides gently back on to his chest

(*Grumblingly*) And don't pretend you don't know sex when you see it.

*Pam lies still. As Joe realizes that he has actually subdued her, his face takes
on an expression of incredulous delight which grows into a beaming, self-
satisfied grin*

Pam (*after a pause; meekly*) Joe!
Joe What?
Pam This is a *new* side to you that I didn't know you'd got.
Joe (*with smug confidence*) Well—what do you think of it?
Pam (*hesitating faintly*) It *does* give me something fresh to think about.
Joe (*suddenly dismayed*) Oh Lord! Do you mean I've started you off on a
new tack?
Pam (*sitting up*) But *really*, Joe, we *must* be sensible about it.
Joe (*bitterly petulant*) All right, then! (*He grabs her head and kisses her
roughly*) Go away and analyse that! (*He sits back and turns his head away
as if severing relations with her*) Only don't be too long about it, or I may
have gone home.

*Pam looks at his averted head for a moment—a faint, tender smile dawning on
her face—then she gently snuggles down to him. Joe looks down at her in
astonishment but otherwise makes no move*

Pam (*after a pause*) Joe—don't let's do any more study tonight.
Joe Uh?
Pam We've *both* had an *aw*fully full day—and we *must* have *some*
relaxation, mustn't we?
Joe (*plaintively*) Yes—well—*I'm* perfectly ready to . . .
Pam (*interrupting*) Let's forget our problems for this evening, shall we?
Let's be gay and silly and heedless for once.
Joe *Ce*rtainly! *I've* no objection to . . .
Pam (*interrupting*) Let's go and sit on the stile and watch the sun go down.
Joe (*tenderly*) Oh, Pam! Really?

Pam kisses him gently and sweetly and jumps to her feet

Pam I'll get a coat.

Pam runs off R

*Joe, looking very pleased with himself, gets to his feet. He takes out a
cigarette, lights it and inhales deeply with the satisfied air of one enjoying
the fullness of life. Humming gently to himself, he wanders up to the radio
and switches it on*

Radio Voice . . . or the later Magnum Concilium . . .
Joe (*switching it off, laughing indulgently*) Good old Magnum Concilium!

Pam enters R. *She is struggling into a light sports coat. Millicent and Paul enter up* RC *from off* L. *Millicent now wears a simple frock. Paul is dressed as before*

Millicent Hullo! We've been watching the sunset. (*She moves to the piano*)
Pam From the stile?
Millicent (*at piano*) Yes.
Joe (*happily*) That's what we're gong to do.
Paul (*coming down* C) Well, you'd better hurry up, or there won't *be* any sunset. (*He sinks rather wearily into the chesterfield and picks up a magazine*)
Millicent Getting a bit chilly, too.

Pam exits up RC *and goes off* L

Joe (*cheerfully*) That won't worry us. (*He grabs his muffler from the piano— then hesitates; to Paul*) I say—it's just occurred to me—*you*'ll be my *father*-in-law, won't you?
Paul (*smiling*) I suppose so—yes.
Joe Well, well, well! Life's full of surprises, isn't it? (*He laughs and goes out up* RC, *then bobs back again; to Millicent, with a glance at Paul*) How're you doing?

Millicent responds with an impatient little gesture and goes off L

Joe exits

Millicent (*coming down to* R *of the chesterfield*) Well—as I was saying—I *was* going back tomorrow, but when Mrs Coot packed up, I suggested to Mrs Dickson that I should stay on for a bit and help—and, of course, she jumped at it. So, you see, it's an ill wind . . .!
Paul You mean you've got a particular reason for wanting to stay on?

Throughout the following scene Millicent's manner, though often constrained, is always earnest and without any hint of coquettishness

Millicent (*looking at him levelly*) That remains to be seen, Mr Dickson.
Paul (*momentarily meeting her eye and becoming vaguely uneasy*) Oh! What about some light in here?
Millicent Don't you think it's rather nice as it is? (*She moves just below the* R *corner of the chesterfield*)
Paul Please yourself! But it won't stay as it is.

Millicent stands like an artless schoolgirl. She speaks with some effort, but is determinedly unafraid to meet Paul's eye

Millicent I know, but—(*she hesitates*)—as a matter of fact, I've got something to say which—I'd *rather* say in a bad light, if you don't mind.
Paul (*uncomprehendingly*) You've got what?
Millicent You see, it's a bit—it's a bit *personal* and I'm not *used* to talking in this sort of way—if you see what I mean.
Paul (*bemused*) Well, I can't say exactly see what you mean, but . . . (*He breaks off*)
Millicent It's about my profession.
Paul Oh!

Millicent I want your advice.

Paul Well, certainly if . . . (*He breaks off and puts down the magazine*)

Millicent As you know—I'm an actress.

Paul I didn't know. Are you a good one?

Millicent Not very. That's the trouble. I'm tight.

Paul You're *what*?

Millicent Tight! That's a term we have for when you're all sort of screwed up inside. (*With suitable clutching movements of the hands*) When you—when you can't *give*. When you *want* to give and feel that you're *cap*able of giving and, and, and just *can't*.

Paul Certainly doesn't sound too good. How come your inside's got into that state?

Millicent Well, that's the point. According to Peter (*as she crosses to* LC)—he's the producer at the repertory company where I work—it's all due to my being—well—inexperienced.

Paul What does he expect at your age?

Millicent But I don't mean *stage* experience. I mean—experience of *life*.

Paul (*indulgently understanding*) Ah!

Millicent He says I shall *never* be any good until I've had an affaire.

Paul (*a little grimly*) He says that, does he?

Millicent Yes—but not with just anybody.

Paul (*ironically*) Oh, not just anybody. Peter's pretty exacting, isn't he?

Millicent No, it's got to be a seasoned man-of-the-world. Somebody who'll know how to create the sort of emotional upheaval that will rack me to the depths of my being and—and kind of loosen everything up.

Paul I see.

Millicent He says it's a crying shame the way my unborn talents are going to waste.

Paul Well, if he's so concerned about it, why doesn't he do a bit of racking himself?

Millicent Oh, he hasn't time for that sort of thing.

Paul But surely—in the interests of art . . .!

Millicent Besides, he's not much older than I am.

Paul I rather suspected that.

Millicent Anyway—much as I admire his genius, I don't like his face.

Paul I'm not surprised. I'm sure it must be revolting.

Millicent So you see, the problem is . . . (*She hesitates and moves to the* L *end of the chesterfield*)

Paul (*interposing*) To find someone suitable.

Millicent (*boggling at the word*) Well, I wouldn't say "*find*" exactly.

Paul Let's be blunt! About forty-five?

Millicent Yes, I should think so.

Paul Plenty of time on his hands?

Millicent It 'ud be an advantage, I suppose.

Paul Presentable?

Millicent Naturally.

Paul And no morals at all!

Millicent Oh no, I didn't mean that.

Paul With a past, then?

Millicent (*doubtfully*) Well—yes.
Paul May I ask—do you like *my* face?
Millicent (*hesitating, then with a note of defiance*) Yes, I do.
Paul (*thoughtfully*) I see. (*Ironically*) And you find all this a bit *per*sonal?
Millicent Matter of fact it—sounds rather worse than I expected.
Paul Hum! Well, is that the worst, or may we have the lights on?

For answer Millicent at once goes up RC *and switches on the lights. Paul idly
picks up the encyclopaedia. Millicent comes down* R *and seats herself demurely
beside Paul, on his* R. *There is a pause during which Paul looks at the book and
Millicent looks anxiously at Paul*

I see somebody's been looking up Peru. (*He turns to the front of the book*)
Huh! Published in eighteen-ninety-eight! That'll be a help.

Slight pause

Millicent Mind you—I'm not en*tire*ly sold on the idea myself.
Paul Eh? (*Looking up*) Oh, you're not?
Millicent No. At the moment I'm—really only feeling my way.
Paul (*looking at the book again*) Ah!
Millicent Meanwhile I—just thought you might like to know about it—for
what it's worth.
Paul I'm extremely grateful to you.
Millicent (*murmuring*) Not at all!

Pause

Haven't you any comment to make?

Paul shuts the book with a bang, lays it aside and hesitates

Paul Look—let's behave like men and women of the world, shall we?
Millicent (*with a note of alarm*) What, *now*?
Paul Yes. Let's say exactly what we mean.
Millicent (*relaxing*) Oh!
Paul You don't *really* want my advice, do you?
Millicent No.
Paul But you're going to get it, all the same. Have you a father?
Millicent Yes.
Paul A strong one?
Millicent (*wonderingly*) Yes.
Paul Go and ask him to spank you.
Millicent (*in a stunned whisper*) I beg your pardon?
Paul Hard!
Millicent (*rising slowly; without resentment*) Oh! Oh, I see! Then you're not
...? You don't ...?
Paul (*rising courteously; quite kindly*) I'm sorry. I'm most deeply
honoured—but I'm not—and I don't.
Millicent (*backing away up* R *and across behind the chesterfield to* C) Well—
there was no harm in mentioning it, was there?
Paul (*politely*) None whatever.

Millicent (*halting; hesitating*) I suppose it's no good saying so now, but . . . (*She breaks off*)
Paul Yes?
Millicent I don't think I really meant it.
Paul I'm quite sure you didn't.
Millicent Believe me, I wouldn't have done it—even for the sake of my art—if I hadn't had very good reasons besides.
Paul I do believe you.

Angela and Charles enter R

Millicent (*stepping forward impulsively, holding out her hand*) May I say that I think you're a very nice man?

Angela moves to the R *arm of the chesterfield. Charles, who is looking very tired, crosses to the piano*

Paul (*taking Millicent's hand*) Thank you!

Angela pauses in some surprise at the sight of Millicent and Paul shaking hands with such formality

Millicent (*to Paul*) And I'm so sorry to have troubled you.
Paul No trouble at all!
Millicent Good-night!
Paul Good-night!

They release hands

   Millicent walks straight out through the door R *without a glance at the others*

Angela stares after her in puzzlement. Paul sinks back into the chesterfield and mops his brow

Charles Well, I'm off! (*He picks up his hat*)

Angela crosses to Charles

Paul Oh, are you? Good-night!
Charles (*to Angela*) Good-night, old girl! (*He kisses her chastely*)
Angela Good-night, Charles!

Charles puts on his hat and starts towards the doors L. *He still has the dish-cloth hanging down his leg*

   (*Solicitously*) Don't do any packing tonight, dear.
Paul (*mischievously*) Mustn't overdo it, old chap.
Charles (*glancing doubtfuly at Paul*) Not likely. (*His hand encounters the dish-cloth and he moves absent-mindedly into the porch tucking it into his pocket*)

   Charles exits L

Paul (*stretching and yawning*) Well, if you don't mind, I think I'll go up. (*He gets to his feet*)

Angela (*coming down* L *of the chesterfield*) Yes, I think so too. I'm *quite* exhausted. I've *put* an apple by your bed, and . . .
Paul (*interrupting; gently*) Angela—did you remember that?
Angela (*coldly*) I *al*ways assume that my guests like an apple. (*She goes up to the door up* RC *and locks it*)
Paul The kids are still out, you know. (*He crosses to the door* R)
Angela Oh! (*She unlocks the door*) What about early-morning tea? Do you still like it at eight?
Paul Yes—still at eight!

Angela stands with her hand on the light switch waiting for Paul to go out

Angela I'll get Pam to bring you a cup.
Paul Thank you! (*He opens the door* R)

Angela switches off the lights. The only illumination comes through the open door. It is now almost dark outside

(*Reminiscently*) Takes you back, doesn't it?
Angela What does?
Paul Going up like this.

Angela switches on the lights again

Angela (*grimly*) I think I'll sit up a little longer, after all.
Paul (*smiling*) Good-night, then!
Angela (*coming down behind the chesterfield; coldly*) Good-night!

   Paul exits R

Angela's expression softens in what is apparently a not unpleasant reverie. This is broken by the sound of voices off

   Pam and Joe enter up RC *from off* L. *Pam is dabbing at her mouth with a handkerchief*

Pam (*crossing down* LC; *angrily*) And don't swear at my family, either!
Joe (*following Pam; protesting*) I *was*n't swearing at your family.
Pam What *did* you say, then?
Joe I said *blood* relations.
Pam (*grumblingly*) Well, anyway . . .! (*She crosses to* R *below the chesterfield, dabbing at her mouth*)
Angela What have you done to your mouth, dear?
Pam (*by the door* R) That fool *kissed* me. Clumsy oaf!

   Pam stamps out R

Angela What *does* she mean?
Joe I forgot to take the cigarette out of my mouth, that's all. (*He throws himself gloomily into the easy chair*)
Angela (*disappointed yet sympathetic*) Oh *Joe*! Oh, you poor darling! (*She moves to him*)
Joe (*a mass of self-pity*) She gets me so nervous, I don't know what I'm doing.
Angela Oh, that *was* a pity. I'm *so* sorry. Is she coming back?

Joe *I* don't know. Damn fine whirlwind lover *I* turned out to be. (*He pulls off his muffler*)

Angela (*comfortingly*) Never mind, dear! We'll think of something else.

Joe reacts to this with a look of alarm

Look, I'll go and see what she's doing, shall I? (*Crossing to* R) Otherwise you won't know whether to go home or not, will you? I expect she's only putting something on it.

Angela exits R

Joe sits glaring after her for a moment. Then he gets to his feet and mooches up to window. After staring into the darkness for a second or two, he wanders down to the chesterfield, picks up "Woman and Home", glances at it and drops it back again. He hesitates uncertainly, then moves to the door R *and listens. As he turns away, his bored eye is caught by the radio. Idly he switches it on*

Radio Voice . . . is sufficiently attested by the clauses of Magna Charta. . . .

Joe (*wildly*) Is it *pos*sible? (*He switches off the radio and turns angrily away muttering*) I've had enough of this. (*He crosses to the easy chair, grabs his muffler and strides with determination to the door up* RC)

Pam enters R

Pam (*running to Joe*) Joe! Joe—don't go for a minute!

Joe (*halting halfway through the door*) What do you want?

Pam I—I've just realized something.

Joe So have I. (*He shuts the door*) It just came to me. (*Advancing aggressively to her*) *Who* the *hell* do you think you are?

Pam (*taken aback*) Wha'? (*She retreats down* LC *before him*)

Joe (*advancing; his face stuck into hers*) Has it occurred to you that all this fuss about who you're going to marry's nothing more than concentrated *egotism on your part?

Pam But, Joe, I . . .

Joe (*interrupting*) What makes you think *your* happiness is so bloody important than you can't take a chance like anyone else?

Pam opens her mouth to reply, but gets no chance

What's it matter if you *are* unhappy, *any*way? What's so special about *you* that you shouldn't be unhappy? *Lots* of people are.

Pam But, Joe, it's not my happiness that I'm thinking about now, really it isn't.

Joe Whose is it, then—generations unborn?

Pam No, dear—yours!

Joe (*breaking away and going to the fireplace*) Well, you can mind your own damn business about my happiness. *I'll* take care of that.

Pam (*following*) But, *Joe*, dear, *listen*, *please*! I've just been talking to Millicent.

Joe (*cooling down; muttering*) Anybody 'ud think . . .

Pam (*interrupting loudly*) She *prac*tically *off*ered herself to him and he snubbed her.

Joe (*irritably*) What are you *talk*ing about?

Pam *Father!* She tested him out and he wouldn't have anything to *do* with her.

Joe Well, what about it? What's that got to do with . . .?

Pam (*interrupting*) Only that it completely confirms what I suspected. He's *not* an outsider: he's a *very nice man.*

Joe (*wearily bitter*) Oh, *I* get it. That'll mean something in *my* life, of *course.*

Pam Well, of course it will, in a way.

Joe (*resignedly*) All right! Go on! What is it—good or bad? *I* don't know. I've lost count. (*He sighs hopelessly and sits on the arm of the easy chair*)

Pam (*reasonably*) Joe—let's be logical for a moment. First of all—I really am convinced that if a girl couldn't live happily with you, there must be something wrong with her.

Joe (*unable to believe his ears*) What?

Pam There *couldn't* be any guile in a man who forgets he's got a cigarette in his mouth.

Joe (*brightening*) Well—that's all right then, isn't it? (*Wearily*) Or isn't it?

Pam No, because . . . (*She hesitates*)

Joe (*subsiding into defeatism again*) No, I thought not.

Pam It looks as though there may be something wrong with *me.*

Joe (*sarcastically*) Oh come! You mustn't get introspective.

Pam (*ignoring this*) I mean—if Mummy couldn't get on with a nice person like Paul, it was obviously her fault. And as I'm so like her, it *does* look as if I might turn out to be difficult to live with *too.*

Joe To tell you the truth, that thought *had* passed across my mind.

Pam (*faintly anxious*) It had?

Joe In fact, for some time I've envisaged a life of suffering and horror that I'm sure I've done *noth*ing to deserve.

Pam (*taking his head and holding it protectively to her bosom*) Then don't worry, darling! If you feel like that, I won't *let* you marry me.

Joe (*somewhat muffled*) But it doesn't *mean* I don't want to marry you. I *do.*

Pam That's what I mean, dear. I'll protect you against yourself.

Joe I don't *want* to be pro . . . (*He breaks off*) Oh, what's the use?

Pam stands for a moment in worried thought

Pam Joe—will you do something for me?

Joe (*muffled and pessimistic*) Is there any choice?

Pam releases his head, takes his hand and draws him to his feet

Pam Go home. (*She moves rapidly to the piano, picks up the prayer-book, returns to Joe and leads him up to* C) Go home, dear—and take this with you. (*She puts the prayer-book in his hand*) Do you read in bed?

Joe (*dully*) I hadn't expected to.

Pam Page two-hundred! "The Solemnization of Matrimony"—read it! Study it! (*She begins winding his muffler about his neck*) Don't—don't come back for a few days! Keep away and ponder it! Hold me in mind while you do so! Realize what it means—in terms of *me.* And then—*then* see what you think. Will you?

Joe (*sighing deeply and resignedly*) Pam—do you know what your mother said?

Pam shakes her head silently

(*Sadly*) She said—"Poor Joe! This was to have been your wedding night."

Pam (*with compassion*) I know, dear. But it's better this way.

Joe reacts with a look of bewildered incredulity

(*Gently*) Good-night! (*She lifts her face to be kissed*)

Joe stoops apathetically to kiss her

(*Warningly*) Mind my mouth!

Joe, about to kiss Pam on the lips, checks himself and imprints a chaste salute on her brow, then turns away

Joe (*muttering gloomily*) What's the odds? Good-night!

He goes slowly and dejectedly out up RC *with the prayer-book, shutting the door behind him. He goes off* L. *Pam locks the door and turns to the window to wave as he passes*

But Joe goes wretchedly out of sight without turning his head

Wearing a rather worried look, Pam begins mechanically performing the final small chores of the night. She goes to the chesterfield and thumps its cushions. Then she collects the encyclopaedia and one or two magazines, bears them to the radio and puts them on the top of it. Idly she flicks on the switch of the radio and moves down to the easy chair. The radio begins to emit the familiar interval signal—the chiming Bow Bells. Pam halts, staring before her with an expression of dawning dismay. Then she opens her mouth wide and begins howling like a schoolgirl

CURTAIN

ACT III

The same. After supper, a week later

It is getting late and is dark outside. All the curtains are drawn. Once again the room is in a state of considerable disorder. Two large cardboard dress-boxes, empty and half open, lie on the floor L of the piano. On the piano are several feminine hats and two or three pairs of shoes. Across the back of the chesterfield lies a man's jacket. On the chesterfield is propped a bag of golf clubs. Another man's jacket is draped over the back of the chair down L

When the CURTAIN *rises Angela is sitting amidst a welter of papers at the desk, writing labels. She wears a house-coat. Millicent, dressed in a light frock and evidently very much in a minor key, is sitting with a work-basket beside her, down L. She is stitching a white collar to a dress*

Angela (*looking at the labels; muttering*) Wanted on voyage. *Not* wanted on voyage. (*Writing*) Sir Charles and Lady ... (*She hesitates*) Oh dear, I do hope I'm doing these right. (*To Millicent*) I suppose *you* don't know how Charles spells his name?

Millicent C—H—A—R ...

Angela (*interrupting*) No dear, I mean his *sur*name. I hardly like to ask him at this stage.

Millicent Let me see, now! A—M ... (*She breaks off*)

There are several heavy thumps off R. *Angela rises, runs across and opens the door,* R

Charles and Paul enter. They are carrying an apparently heavy cabin trunk. Charles is in front. He is dressed in grey flannel slacks and a pullover. Paul wears a loose tweed suit. Both are in their shirtsleeves. Both (particularly Charles) are overheated, out of breath and exhausted

At Paul's entrance Millicent drops her work in her lap and follows him everywhere with sadly adoring eyes. Angela leads the way across, below the chesterfield

Paul (*quite cheerfully*) What have you *got* in this thing?

Angela Is it heavy, dear? I'm so sorry. Put it down here, will you? (*She indicates a position down* C)

Paul and Charles begin laboriously to lower the trunk

(*Considering*) No, I think over there. (*She indicates a position up* C)

Paul and Charles carry the trunk up C *and deposit it against the downstage side of the piano*

Thank you *so* much! (*She moves to the chesterfield and begins tying a label on the golf clubs*)

Charles, mopping his brow, crosses above the chesterfield straight to the drinks buffet and takes out a glass

Paul (*crossing to the door* R; *to Charles*) Here—we're not finished yet, you know. There's another one upstairs.

Charles (*dismayed*) Another? (*To Angela*) But you've already sent a . . .

Angela (*interrupting*) We're not going for the weekend, dear.

Paul (*with a faint, mischievous smile*) Marriage is apt to go on a long time, Charles.

Charles (*slightly irritable*) I *know* it is, old chap. *I* know. Why does everyone keep on telling me that?

Charles replaces the glass with a not particularly good grace and exits R

Angela (*grimly*) That'll be *Pam* again.

Paul (*sympatheticaly*) Poor old Charles! He's tired. I expect the excitement gets him down a bit—at his age.

Paul throws a quick glance at Angela and exits R

A small, thoughtful frown momentarily clouds Angela's brow. She props the golf bag on the chesterfield and crosses to the desk

Angela (*sitting*) Where *is* Pam, anyway?

Millicent The last *I* saw of her, she was still in her room.

Angela (*with a sigh*) How she can sit there calmly reading "The Decline and Fall" with everybody else reducing themselves to a state of collapse, I don't know.

Millicent I think it's her conscience. She says it won't *let* her help.

Angela But it's been going on the whole week. Nobody's conscience could be as persistent as that. (*She tries to turn her attention to the labels*) Let me see, now . . .! (*Muttering*) The pig-skin suitcase—because that's got my . . . So I *must* have that. Then there's the—er . . . (*To Millicent*) *I* wouldn't say "at his age" exactly, would you?

Millicent I beg your pardon?

Angela Charles! He doesn't strike *you* as—erm—as elderly or anything, does he?

Millicent No, I was only saying last night—*I* think he's very young-looking.

Angela (*mildly gratified*) Do you, dear?

Pam enters R. *She wears a shirt and slacks. In sharp contrast to all the others, she seems fresh, leisurely and unruffled*

At Pam's appearance Angela makes signs to Millicent to discontinue the discussion

Millicent (*continuing, oblivious*) Yes, I'm *sure* he must be older than he looks. Pam doesn't think he *can* be.

Pam (*lounging across to* C) Who's this?

Millicent Sir Charles! I was just saying . . .

Pam (*interrupting*) If he's older than he looks he must be *very* well preserved—that's all *I* say.

Angela (*suspiciously*) How do you mean?

Pam (*moving behind the easy chair*) Look at the way he humps those trunks about, for instance. He must have the arteries of a man of forty-five.

Angela (*turning to get on with her work*) Well, it's surprising to hear *you* admit that he's even healthy.

Pam Probably find he's got an expectation of life of thirty years yet. As a matter of fact, I was working it out, and ...

Angela (*turning and interrupting forcefully*) Pam, I will *not* listen to anything else that you've worked out.

Pam (*moving to Angela*) Mummy, you *must* listen. I won't *have* you shutting your eyes to things like this. Thirty years is something over ten thousand days and nights. Ten thousand! Do you realize what that means?

Angela opens her mouth to speak, but gets no opportunity

No, of *course* you don't. You haven't *thought* about it. Supposing he calls you "old girl" on an average only twice every twenty-four hours—that's more than *twenty-thousand times*. It's an ap*pall*ing thought. But *you* haven't let it enter your *head, have* you?

Angela I've let it enter my head to the extent of wondering why you haven't brought it up before.

Pam (*beginning argumentatively*) Mummy, look ...

Angela (*rising; interrupting firmly*) Pam—for a week I've had to endure your nagging. For a week ...

Pam crosses to the chesterfield and begins idly examining the label on the golf bag

... you've done nothing but rake up statistics and suggest every conceivable shortcoming that might possibly be possessed by Charles or by Peru. *Now* I suppose you're getting ready to say "why take your clubs? The Peruvians haven't even got a golf-course."

Pam (*behind the chesterfield*) I don't see why you want 'em on voyage, anyway.

Angela, shaken by this, snatches up a fresh label and crosses to the front of the chesterfield

Angela (*snatching up the clubs*) There! You see? I *knew* I'd do something like that. (*Pettishly tearing the label off the clubs and crossing with the clubs to the easy chair*) *All* you achieve by these incessant obstructions is to make me so confused that I ... (*Suddenly vehement*) What *good* do you think you're doing anyway? Can't you see that if I *were* undecided about Charles ...

Pam (*interrupting eagerly*) Oh, Mummy, *are* you?

Angela No, of *course* I'm not. I said "if". But *if* I *were*—don't you realize you're doing the very thing to make me go through with it? If only to annoy *you*. (*She sniffs emotionally*) You know what I am. (*She sits in the easy chair with the clubs beside her*)

Pam instantly contrite, runs impulsively to Angela, throws herself on her knees, and encircles her with her arms

Pam Yes, I know what you are, darling. That's why I love you so much. (*Becoming emotional*) That's why I want you to be happy. That's why I'm making such a little beast of myself.

Angela (*responding immediately; taking Pam in her arms*) Pam, darling!

Pam (*crying*) But I don't en*joy* doing it—*real*ly I don't. I *hate* being out of favour.

Millicent is quite unimpressed by the scene. Her frequent tragic sighs and her close application to her work suggest that she is absorbed in her own sad thoughts

Angela (*crying*) Never mind, my pet—you follow your conscience as much as you please.

Pam No, Mummy, no! You marry anyone you like. Don't take any notice of ... (*She breaks off*)

The telephone bell rings. Angela and Pam release each other. Angela rises, hands Pam the fresh label and, sniffing spasmodically, goes to the phone. Pam gets to her feet, blows her nose, sits in the easy chair and begins unobtrusively to tie the label on the clubs

Angela (*into the phone; still shaken by deep emotion*) Yes? ... Oh, Mrs Bedford dear! ... Yes. ... You've just heard what? ... Oh, about my. ... Yes, it's to-morrow. Isn't it lovely? (*She gasps convulsively*) ... Yes, it *has* been rather a rush, but ... What? ... Twelve-thirty at the church, dear. At least, that's the present arrangement. ... No, no, none at all. I don't know why I said that. ... Well, hardly a reception. Just a few close friends at the *Red Lion* afterwards. ... Oh, *did*n't we? We *meant* to ask you. Of *course* you must come. It'll be *such* fun. (*She sniffs spasmodically*) ... I think it's the wire, dear. You sound funny, too. ... Oh, Pam's *very* well, thank you.

Pam throws Angela a warning look

(*Hurriedly*) I—I mean she's as well as can be expected. See you to-morrow, then! ... Yes. Good-night! (*She replaces the receiver and sits on the stool*)

Pam (*rising and putting the golf bag down against the back of the easy chair*) There! *Not* wanted on voyage! Would you like a cup of tea, Mummy?

Angela A little later, dear.

Pam (*hesitating slightly*) Are you going to be there long?

Angela Why? Do you want to use the phone?

Pam (*jauntily*) No, no! No hurry! Let me see, now! What else can I do to help? (*She considers momentarily, then crosses towards the door* R)

Mrs Mandrake enters R. *She is dressed as in the previous scene. She looks more woebegone than ever. With one hand she holds a screwed-up handkerchief to her nose. In the other she carries a large bunch of small keys*

(*She meets Mrs Mandrake near the door and pauses; in a low*

voice) Mandy! Do try to be a little more cheerful—for Mummy's sake—
there's a dear.

Pam exits R

Mrs Mandrake stares after Pam in some surprise

Mrs Mandrake (*crossing up stage towards the piano*) I've found another
bunch. (*She holds out the keys*)

Angela Oh, good! (*She rises, moves to the trunk and takes the keys*) Now—
some of these must fit *some*thing, surely. (*She crouches and begins trying to
fit keys to the lock of the trunk*)

Watching Angela above the chesterfield, Mrs Mandrake's emotion mounts

Now, remember Mandy—milkman—hens—Mr Atkins—laundry—
sweep—tool-shed—erm, carpets—fruit and—er . . .

Mrs Mandrake (*wretchedly*) Moth-balls!

Angela Yes, moth-balls! Now, is there anything else you want to discuss?
Because, if so, *don't* leave it till the morning.

Mrs Mandrake I don't think so. We've *never* been separated before, Miss
Angela.

Angela I know, dear, but it's only till Pam gets married—then you can come
out to us.

Mrs Mandrake How am I to know she'll *ever* get married?

Angela Well, it's *nearly* happened once al*ready*—so it must be on the cards.
Now do be a dear and get on with that ironing!

Mrs Mandrake crosses towards the door R

Mrs Mandrake (*halting*) Am I to understand that Mr Paul will be staying
on?

*Now Millicent's attention is really arrested. She drops her work in her lap and
sits up*

Angela (*still struggling with keys*) Just for a week or so, dear. He's going to
help with business—money matters and things.

Mrs Mandrake And Miss Millicent?

Angela Yes, she'll be here too.

Mrs Mandrake (*continuing to the door*) Well, I suppose you know what
you're doing—but I can't be everywhere at once, you know.

Mrs Mandrake exits R

Angela (*in surprise*) Now, what does she mean by that?

Millicent (*with a note of bitterness*) I think she has an idea that Mr Dickson
is not to be trusted with young women.

Pam enters R. *She cheerfully lugs a large and apparently heavy suitcase*

Pam (*crossing to the piano*) They're having trouble with the trunk. It's bust
open.

Angela (*horrified*) You don't mean it's emptied out?

Pam (*reassuringly*) Not *all* of it, dear.

Angela Oh, *what* a week! (*She crosses towards the door* R)

Pam (*putting the suitcase on top of the trunk*) *I'll* see to it, Mummy.

Angela (*halting; harassed*) Pam dear—*please* don't start helping now. If you do, I shall only think it's because you've changed your tactics.

Pam (*complainingly*) Look, Mummy—first I mustn't *not* help. Now I mustn't *help*. What *am* I to do?

Angela (*uncertainly*) Well, if you *must* help, do it in a *nor*mal sort of way. If you're osten*ta*tious about it, it'll have the same effect as the other thing—don't you *see*?

Angela exits R

Pam (*with a gesture of despair*) You see what frightfully inconsistent women we are! What chance has a simple soul like Joe to cope with that sort of thing?

Millicent, again seemingly sunk in her work, does not even trouble to look up

(*She goes to the telephone and lifts the receiver. Into the phone*) Ilcombe seven-one-seven! (*She pauses. To Millicent*) He can't *still* be out. (*Suddenly, into the phone*) Oh, hullo, Joe! . . . Pam! Where have you been all the week? . . . But I only said a few days, dear, I didn't say . . . Well, of course it matters. I—I want to know what you . . . No, it's *not* a matter of delivering a report, Joe. Don't put it like that! I want to *see* you. Besides—Millicent overheard Charles saying that it looked as if—as if you'd buzzed off for good. . . . I know it's none of his damn business, but—we don't want people saying things like that, do we? . . . *Do* come over, Joe! . . . Yes, now! (*She replaces the receiver; excitedly*) He's coming.

Pam runs across to the door R *and exits*

Millicent bites off her thread, puts the needle and thimble in the work-basket, rises and shakes out the dress

Angela enters R

Angela (*coming below the chesterfield*) They seem to be managing all right. Oh dear. I don't know *when* I've been so tired. (*She sinks into the chesterfield*) Finished?

For answer Millicent crosses to the L *end of the chesterfield and hands the dress to Angela*

Oh, thank you, dear! That's lovely!

Millicent Mrs Dickson!

Angela (*examining the dress*) Yes?

Millicent Would you mind very much if I *did*n't stay on?

Angela (*looking up in surprise*) No, dear, of course not, but—why, is anything wrong?

Millicent Yes. (*She hesitates*) I'm in love with *Mr* Dickson.

Angela You're what?

Millicent I've tried to conceal it, but . . . (*She breaks off*)

Angela (*sympathetically*) You poor child! How did *that* happen?

Millicent Well, it serves me right, really. You see, I—made advances to him.

Angela (*incredulously*) You made advances?

Millicent Yes. It wasn't a very nice thing to do, but I—thought I'd sort of kill two birds with one stone—discredit him for Pam's sake and—improve my acting. So I . . . (*She breaks off*)

Angela (*bewildered, but kindly*) I'm not quite sure that I know what you're talking about, dear—but what did *he* do? That's the important thing.

Millicent He . . . (*She hesitates*)

Angela (*anxiously encouraging*) Yes?

Millicent He told me to go and get spanked.

Angela He re*pell*ed you?

Millicent Yes—with contumely.

Angela (*relaxing*) Oh! (*She smiles faintly to herself*)

Millicent It was—beautiful.

Angela Uh?

Millicent In that moment I saw him for what he is—strong—noble—*clean*!

Angela (*with an illogical note of pride*) He *is* rather attractive, isn't he?

Millicent (*dramatically*) Since then—living under the same roof with him—seeing him every day—watching him eat—hearing him laugh—sitting opposite his dear, wise, patient face—it's been terrible, Mrs Dickson—and I don't think I could stand another day of it. So if he's going to stay on . . .

Mrs Mandrake enters R

Mrs Mandrake (*putting her head round the door*) The *boil*er's gone out now.

Angela Oh, heavens! (*Getting to her feet*) Mandy, we *can't* go without baths to-morrow. (*She puts down the dress and moves to Millicent; kindly*) You go when you like, dear. (*She kisses her*) I know just how you feel. (*She turns and crosses to the door* R)

Millicent (*in gentle sympathy*) You would, of course. (*She turns away*)

Angela double-takes this, hesitates as if to ask Millicent what she means, thinks better of it and continues to the door. Mrs Mandrake withdraws before her

Mrs Mandrake exits R

Angela (*as she passes through the door*) I'll get one of the men.

Angela exits R

Millicent stands bleakly for a moment, then her eyes move round to the jacket on the back of the chesterfield. She goes to it, picks it up, gazes wistfully at it, strokes it, kisses it and tenderly crushes it to her bosom. There are several heavy thumps off R. *Millicent hurriedly puts down the jacket, runs to the door* R *and opens it*

Paul and Charles enter R. *They carry another large trunk and are visibly exhausted. Paul comes first*

Millicent fixes her yearning gaze on Paul. The trunk is carried across in silence to the piano and, with many grunts, deposited on top of the other luggage. Millicent follows to up C. *Both men stand panting*

Paul (*to Charles*) Drink?

Charles (*dully*) No, I've got to go and do that damn boiler now.

Charles shakily crosses to the door R, *mopping his neck, and exits*

Paul puts the golf-clubs on top of the trunks, then comes wearily down C *and crosses to the buffet. Millicent follows silently at his heels. Paul begins to mix himself a drink*

Millicent (*sympathetically*) You look *so* hot. (*She gazes at the back of his neck*)

Paul starts at the sound of her voice almost in his ear

Paul I am, a bit.

Millicent Don't you think you ought to have your coat on? (*She moves to the jacket on the chesterfield and picks it up*)

Paul Oh, I don't know.

Millicent (*going to him with the jacket*) *Please*! You don't want to catch a chill.

Paul (*looking over his shoulder*) That's Charles' anyway.

Millicent *What*?

Paul Mine's over there. (*He indicates the armchair down* L, *and crosses below the chesterfield to* C)

Millicent Oh! (*She throws Charles' jacket with spiteful violence on to the floor, runs across to the armchair down* L, *picks up Paul's jacket, crosses to him with it and helps him on with it, gazing with adoration at the back of his neck*)

Paul Thanks! (*Holding his glass, he sinks with a groan into the easy chair and closes his eyes*)

There is a pause

Millicent (*moving to* R *of the easy chair*) Mr Dickson!

Paul Um?

Millicent I'm going.

Paul (*opening his eyes*) I beg your pardon?

Millicent I'm going away. I'm not staying on after all.

Paul Well, I must say I'm not surprised. (*Yawning*) I'm getting a bit sick of sausage-rolls myself.

Millicent (*intensely*) It isn't that. I'd live on sausage-rolls for ever if—(*she breaks off*)—I just thought it best.

Paul (*mystified*) Oh! (*He drinks*)

Millicent hesitates, then steps forward

Millicent So, good-bye!

Paul (*surprised*) You're not going *now*, are you?

Millicent No, but—in the morning there'll be so many people and—there may not be another opportunity and I—I wanted it to be . . . (*She breaks off*)

Paul (*getting to his feet*) Well, goodbye then!

They join hands

Millicent (*gulpingly*) It's been *won*derful knowing you.

Paul (*vaguely*) Has it?
Millicent Good,bye!
Paul (*shaking her hand*) Good-bye!
Millicent (*in a tragic whisper*) Good-bye!
Paul (*shaking her hand*) Good-bye!

Millicent still lingers with her hand in his. Paul shakes her hand once again in silence

> *Millicent releases her hand, turns and goes out* RC *and off* L *without a backward glance*

Paul stares after Millicent with a puzzled frown for a moment. Then he shrugs, moves R, *picks up Charles' jacket, throws another perplexed look after Millicent, puts the jacket on the chesterfield and himself collapses into it with closed eyes*

> *Joe enters up* RC *from off* L. *He enters backwards and pauses in the doorway as if looking in the direction of someone he has just encountered outside*

Paul (*opening his eyes, and looking over his shoulder*) Hullo, Joe!
Joe (*turning with a slight start*) Oh—hullo! (*He comes down stage to the back of the chesterfield*)
Paul Haven't seen much of you lately.
Joe (*laboriously*) No, I've—er—I've had one or two things to—er ... (*He moves to* C)
Paul (*interrupting mercifully*) Have a drink!
Joe (*hesitating*) Well, I don't know whether I should really. I've—er—matter of fact I've just come from the *Red Lion*. (*He sniggers. he has indeed had several drinks. He is not very noticeably affected, but his natural reticence is, to some extent, undermined*)
Paul Another one won't hurt you. Help yourself!
Joe (*giggling*) D'you really think I ought?
Paul Go on!
Joe Well—just a little one, eh? (*He crosses slightly unsteadily to the buffet and begins mixing a whisky and soda*) I say—what's the matter with young Millicent?
Paul (*hesitating slightly*) Tell you the truth, I've rather wondered about that myself. But why do *you* ask?
Joe Just met her outside. (*He jerks his head towards the door up* RC) Said she was on her way to take "one last look at the stile".
Paul The stile?
Joe Yes—you know—where you sat and watched the sunset that evening.
Paul But, what's the idea?
Joe I dunno. Sounds daft to me. (*As he crosses to* C) I mean, why should anyone want to look at a stile?
Paul (*thoughtfully*) Tell me—does she stand and stare at you and—keep on shaking you by the hand?
Joe No—I don't think so—why?
Paul I was just wondering. Perhaps the poor kid's not quite right in the head.

Joe Ooo—I think she's only artistic.
Paul I don't know so much. If you knew some of the things that have been going on here . . .!
Joe Why, what's she been . . . (*Wisely*) Oh yes, of course!
Paul What do you mean "oh yes of course"?
Joe I was forgetting.
Paul What?
Joe That *would* seem a bit strange to you—coming from a girl of her sort.
Paul (*getting slightly aggravated*) What 'ud seem strange?
Joe *You* know. The—er—(*he sniggers*)—the attempt on your virtue.
Paul (*sitting forward; ominously*) Would you mind making yourself clear?
Joe (*incredulously*) D'you mean to say you don't *know*?
Paul No, I do *not* know.
Joe No, I suppose you wouldn't. (*He laughs*) Oh, this'll make you laugh, like a drain. It's a *riot*. (*He takes a drink and sits confidentially on the* L *end of the chesterfield*) You know last week—when you told Millicent where she got off.
Paul Yes, *I* know—but how do *you* know?
Joe Pam told me.
Paul And who told Pam?
Joe Millicent, I think.
Paul (*grimly*) I see. Well—go on! I'm not laughing yet.
Joe She didn't *mean* it. It was *staged*.
Paul You mean, it was a put-up job?
Joe Of *course* it was. She would have been scared out of her pants if you'd—reacted.
Paul (*quite quietly*) And what lay behind this merry prank?
Joe Eh?
Paul (*suddenly losing his temper; loudly*) Why did she *do* it, you fool?
Joe (*rising; startled*) Look—I hope I haven't said too much. I don't want to . . .
Paul (*interrupting angrily*) You haven't said *enough*. *Why* was it staged?
Joe Well—I don't want to . . .
Paul (*jumping to his feet and advancing on Joe aggressively; interrupting*) Look here! Are you going to tell me why respectable young women should lure me with indelicate offers they don't mean—or have I got to knock your block off?
Joe (*backing away in alarm to* L *of the easy chair*) Tell you the truth—I never *could* follow it exactly my*self*, but . . . (*He hesitates*)
Paul (R *of the easy chair; menacingly*) Go on! Go on!
Joe Well—at the time there seemed to be some damn silly idea that it might encourage Pam to—to stop acting the goat if you could be induced to—er—to live up to your reputation.
Paul Which was *what*?
Joe (*uncomfortably*) Well—of being a bit of a—wolf.
Paul So it was a *trap*, was it?
Joe Mind you, I never . . .
Paul (*interrupting*) And they were *all* in it! *Right*! (*Striding to the buffet*) Where *is* the little beast? *I'll* give her a leg up with her acting.

Joe (*uncomprehendingly*) Eh? (*He comes down* C)

Paul plonks down his glass and turns

Paul I'll call her bluff. *I'll* teach her a lesson she won't forget in a hurry.
She'll be playing *char*acter parts after the jolt *I* give her. (*He goes up to
door up* RC, *halts, turns and points at Joe*) And if you marry into *this*
family, young man, you're a bigger bloody fool than I think you are—and
that's saying a good deal.

Paul goes out, slamming the door, and goes off L

Joe (*quite shaken, gaping after Paul*) Gosh! (*Suddenly he drains his glass,
then crosses rapidly to the buffet and refills it. After another pull he moves
up to the door* R *and listens*)

Charles enters R. *He now has a black smear across his face*

*Joe draws nervously aside up stage and Charles, without seeing him, comes
straight down to the buffet and pours out a neat whisky. He takes a gulp, then
falls into the chesterfield and seems to lapse instantly into coma*

(*After an uncertain pause*) I say . . .!

Charles (*starting violently*) Eh? (*He looks over his shoulder*) Oh! (*He relaxes*)
Oh, it's you!

Joe Haven't seen Pam, have you?

Charles (*wearily*) Haven't seen anything much for the past hour or so.
Don't think I've been able to focus properly. (*He closes his eyes*)

Joe (*coming down* R *of the chesterfield*) Takes it out of you, doesn't it—
getting married?

Charles (*feelingly*) I never knew.

Joe (*seating himself on the* R *end of the chesterfield; ruminatively*) Yes—there
are lots of things about marriage you don't realize until you start swatting
it up. Matter of fact, that's what I've been doing all the week. (*He turns to
Charles impressively*) Do *you* know . . .?

Charles (*opening his eyes and interrupting pleadingly*) Look! Don't bother
me with that now—there's a good chap! Have a drink or something! Oh,
you've got one. (*He closes his eyes again*)

Joe looks at his glass and drains it

Joe Well! (*He rises*) Perhaps just a . . . (*He goes to the buffet, helps himself to
neat whisky, returns, sits on the chesterfield beside Charles, on his* R, *and
remains in contemplation a moment*) So this is your last night as a
bachelor—eh? (*He slaps Charles on the thigh*)

Charles starts and groans but makes no reply

(*After a slight pause*) Funny to think that this time last week, that's what
I was thinking.

There is no response from Charles

(*After a slight pause*) Just shows you, doesn't it? (*He drinks*)

Silence

(*After a slight pause*) I say—would you mind telling me something? Mind you, I wouldn't ask *anyone* this—but as you'll be my step-father-in-law or something, if everything goes all right, I don't mind . . .

Charles (*opening his eyes; interrupting*) What do you mean "if everything goes all right"?

Joe Well, after all, we're only en*gaged*, and in Pam's case . . .

Charles (*interrupting; relaxing*) Oh, I see what you mean. (*Resignedly*) Well—what is it?

Joe What do *you* think's the matter with her?

Charles Matter with her?

Joe Yes.

Charles Pam?

Joe Yes.

Charles Wants a damn good hiding.

Joe No—seiously, I mean! (*He rises and crosses to* C)

Charles (*settling himself full length on the chesterfield, his head at the* R *end*) I *am* serious. What *she* lacks . . . This is no reflection on *An*gela, mind you!

Joe Oh, no.

Charles What she lacks is a father's guiding hand.

Joe That's not *all, sure*ly?

Charles If dear old Paul had had the bringing up of her, she would have been a different girl. But as it is—there's only one thing that'll do her any good.

Joe A damn good . . .?

Charles Yes—and not where you knock any *teeth* out *either*. (*He empties his glass and closes his eyes again*)

Joe (*much impressed*) Well, I'm blowed! (*Wandering up* R) Course, *he* seems to think it's something deeper than that. But then, I suppose he would as it's his guiding hand that's missing. (*He empties his glass*)

There is no response from Charles

(*After a slight pause, coming down* R) Still, I must say it shook me a bit—coming from *him*, because if *any*body ought to know . . .

Charles (*opening his eyes; interrupting irritably*) What are you talking about now?

Joe (*bending over the end of the chesterfield so that he looks into Charles' face upside-down*) Old Dickson! I say it sh——

Charles (*interrupting*) *What* shook you?

Joe Well—telling me not to marry Pam!

Charles (*in surprise*) He told you *not* to? (*He sits up*)

Joe (*straightening up*) Yes, he said if I married into this family, I should be a bigger . . . I should be very ill-advised.

Charles (*badly shaken*) Paul said *that*?

Joe But I don't take much notice of it because—after all, he's been unlucky with one of 'em and he's bound to be a bit prejudiced.

Charles (*vaguely*) Yes. (*He holds out his glass*) Get me another, will you?

Joe takes Charles' glass and goes to the buffet

Joe (*pouring whisky; meditatively*) Funny thing—life! Soda?

Charles No, thanks!

Joe leaves his own glass at the buffet, hands Charles his drink and wanders up stage and across to LC, *pondering*

Joe Pity they had to part, you know. Might have saved *all* this trouble. Nice couple, too!

Charles lifts his glass and is about to drink

   Pam enters R

Charles remains apprehensively transfixed with his glass raised

Pam (*at the door*) Oh, Charles! Mummy says she's *ter*ribly sorry to disturb you again, but *could* you just come through a minute?

   Without replying, Charles sighs deeply, drags himself to his feet, puts down his drink on the buffet and goes out dully R

   (*With an apologetic little smile as Charles passes her*) In the cellar! (*She closes the door and turns to Joe*)

Both have an air of restraint

Pam (*moving below the chesterfield; diffidently*) 'Lo, Joe!
Joe Hullo!
Pam (*after a slight pause; in a small voice*) I'm *ter*ribly glad to see you.
Joe (*awkwardly*) Oh—good! (*He pauses slightly, then produces the prayer-book from his pocket*) I—er—I've brought this back.
Pam (*advancing to him*) Oh! (*She takes the book*) Thanks! (*She hesitates*) Did you—er—did you do what we . . .? (*She breaks off*)
Joe (*gloomily*) Yes.
Pam Thoroughly?
Joe Yes.

Pam hesitates, then looks at the ground

Pam And—er—and have you . . .? (*She breaks off*)
Joe (*uneasily*) No, I can't say I have.
Pam (*looking up disappointedly*) Joe!

   Paul enters through the porch. He is still looking furious. He slams the door behind him and strides straight across below the chesterfield to the door R

Joe (*to Paul*) Find her?
Paul Not yet. (*Grimly*) She'll be back. She'll be back.

   Paul goes out R, *slamming the door*

Joe (*calling after him pleasantly*) Probably went on to say good-bye to something else.
Pam (*in surprise*) Who's he looking for?
Joe Millicent.
Pam Seems put out about something.
Joe *I'*ll say he's put out. Matter of fact, I'm glad to see him back. I was afraid he was going to do her a mischief.

Pam Mischief! What sort of mischief?

Joe Well, I don't know exactly—but you know last week when Millicent made a pass at him?

Pam Yes.

Joe Well—(*he hesitates*)—somehow or other he found *out* about that.

Pam (*unimpressed*) Is that all? (*She moves up* C *and puts the prayer-book on the piano*)

Joe (*moving to the door up* RC; *excitedly*) *All!* If you'd seen the way he went off through that door swearing he was going to teach her a lesson and call her bluff and God knows what, *you'd* . . .

Pam (*coming down to the fireplace, interrupting*) But that's only a matter of a little tactful explanation, Joe.

Joe I don't know so much. (*Gesticulating towards the door up* RC) If you'd *seen* the way *that* man . . .

Pam (*interrupting*) Joe! You've got something *much* more important to tell me about, than that.

Joe (*suddenly gloomily solemn again*) Yes, I know.

Pam Well?

Joe hesitates uneasily then moves down C

(*With a note of impatience*) *Joe—are* you going to marry me or *not*?

Joe (*crossing to her, in slow surprise*) Is *that* what I'm supposed to have been deciding?

Pam Of *course*! What did you *think* you were deciding?

Joe Whether I should be able to stick it if I *did*.

Pam Well, that's the same thing, isn't it?

Joe (*warily*) *Oh* no, you don't! You're not going to shove all the responsibility on to me. I'm not going to have you coming to me in about thirty years' time and saying "there you are, you see, it's your fault, you did the deciding". If ever I marry you, it'll be because we've *both* decided.

Pam But I've already *said* I'm satisfied about you. All *you*'ve got to decide is whether you're satisfied about *me*.

Joe And that's exacty what I *can't* decide.

Pam Joe—what have you been *do*ing all the week?

Joe (*pathetically*) Pam—I've arranged three-and-a-half hours a *day* on it. I've *parsed* it and *para*phrased it. I've searched my soul and stared at it till I see *double*—and *still* I don't know.

Pam (*becoming subdued*) I see. (*She looks worried, moves to the armchair down* L *and sits*) Don't you *want* to marry me any more?

Joe (*quite violently*) Of *course* I want to marry you. But what I *can't* do is guarantee that I'm going to *like* it.

Pam (*downcast*) No—I see that.

Joe *Or* carry it out—if it comes to that! All this comforting and honouring and keeping and having and holding and whatnot! (*He takes a piece of paper with notes from his pocket and stands over her at the fireplace*) Take "honour" for instance! Do you know what the Dictionary of Synonyms says about "honour"? (*He reads*) "Exalt, magnify, glorify, dignify, elevate, reverence, respect, revere, worship, venerate, adore"!

And that's only *one* of 'em, mind you. To be applied to *you* of all people!
(*He moves to the easy chair*) See what I mean? (*He sits*)
Pam (*without resentment; dispiritedly*) So we're not really much further
advanced, are we?
Joe No, and what's more, I don't see how we *can* be. Seems to me, all you
can do is mean it when you say it, and after that do your best.
Pam (*deeply impressed*) Oh, but, Joe—I think that's *lovely*.
Joe (*suspiciously*) How d'you mean?
Pam (*looking at him admiringly*) I've never heard *any*thing so beautifully
put.
Joe (*surprised and gratified*) What—"mean it when you say it and . . ."
Pam (*intervening*) ". . . after that do your best". I think it's the most *clear*-
sighted thing I ever heard *any*one say.
Joe (*smirking modestly*) Think so?
Pam No-one can do *more* than their best, Joe, can they?
Joe Course not!
Pam Well *I* will, and I know *you* will.
Joe (*warily*) So what?
Pam (*with shining eyes*) That puts everything *right*, my darling.
Joe (*hesitating mistrustfully*) Look! Let's get this straight. (*Slowly*) Do you
mean . . .?
Pam (*rising and running to him*) Oh, Joe . . .! (*She flings herself down at his
feet, clings to his leg and rests her head on it*) We'll get on to the vicar first
thing in the morning and see if he can make it a *dou*ble wedding—shall
we? Shall we, Joe?

Joe gawks silently

(*Hugging his knee*) Oh, my blessed, I can't tell you how sorry I am for all
the trouble and worry I've put you to. But you'll have to face up to it, you
know. I *am* difficult.
Joe (*who is finding it hard to think of suitable things to say*) Oh, I don't
know.
Pam Oh yes, I am. And I shall go *on* making you unhappy from time to
time. But I shall make you happy too, I promise you. I *prom*ise I shall.
Joe Oh, I'm sure you will—every now and again. (*He is still quite dazed, but
delight is beginning to dawn*)
Pam After a time I expect you'll learn how to deal with me—and then it'll
be easier. What I *real*ly need, you know, is a firm hand.
Joe Oh! (*He glances at the chesterfield as if connecting this with what Charles
has just told him*)
Pam Yes—I expect you could have avoided *all* this bother, if only you'd
known how.
Joe (*in polite surprise*) Go on!
Pam If you'd suddenly said, for instance—"Look here, I've had enough of
this, I've got my car outside and we're going to elope"—I should
probably have come with you like a lamb. I'm *like* that, you know.
Joe (*still politely surprised*) Good Lord!
Pam (*exuberantly*) Oh Joe, I'm so happy! (*She reaches up with both hands,
draws his head down and kisses him on the mouth. But as she releases him,*

some of her ardour seems to have left her. She sits slowly back on her heels looking at him as if suddenly disturbed about something)

Joe is now beaming

Joe—would you mind doing that again? *(She lifts her face)*
Joe *(accommodatingly)* Sure! *(He leans down and kisses her)*
This time Pam keeps her arms at her sides
Pam *(after a slight pause during which she seems to appraise the kiss)* Joe dear—have you been drinking?
Joe *(startled)* Eh?
Pam *(gently insistent)* Have you, Joe?
Joe *(with a note of defiance)* Yes—what about it?
Pam Oh! *(She gets thoughtfully to her feet)*
Joe Have you any objection?
Pam None at all, dear, only . . . *(She breaks off and moves pensively away to* c)
Joe *(getting aggressive)* Only what?
Pam Where?
Joe What do you mean "where"?
Pam Where did you have it?
Joe *(indicating buffet)* Here!
Pam Anywhere else?
Joe Well, I had a couple of games of darts at the *Red Lion.*
Pam Is that where you've been when I haven't been able to get you in the evenings?
Joe I expect so—yes.
Pam Oh!
Joe *(defiantly)* Every night this week, if you want to know.
Pam Why?
Joe *Why!*
Pam Yes. I mean, you never *used* to. Not *reg*ularly like that. Why do you suddenly start going to the *Red Lion?*
Joe Because I was fed-up and had nothing to do, I suppose.
Pam I see.
Joe *(rising resentfully)* Now, look here! I tell you flat—if you're going to start telling me when I can . . .
Pam *(interrupting earnestly)* Joe, darling—*I* don't mind—*hon*estly I don't. It's just that . . . *(She breaks off)*
Joe *What?*
Pam *(almost apologetically)* Well, I do think it's something we ought to *think* about.
Joe *(sinking hopelessly back into the easy chair)* Oh, my Gawd! *(He seizes his head in his hands)*
Pam *(going to him; argumentatively)* I mean—if you're going to start *tur*ning to the *bot*tle every time you're bored or fed-up . . .! Well, it *is* a thing that . . .! I mean, look what happened to Mandy's marriage and— and Mrs Coot's and . . . *(She breaks off)*

Angela enters R

Angela (*putting her head in at the door*) Pam, dear—can you come a minute?
Oh, hullo, Joe!
Joe (*half rising with a bleak attempt at a smile; dully*) Hullo!
Angela (*to Joe; fatuously*) You came to see us then, at last?
Joe Yes.
Angela That's right! (*She withdraws*)

Joe sinks back into the chair. Pam crosses to the door R

Angela exits R

Pam (*turning at the door; full of concern*) But don't *worry* about it, dear.

Pam exits R

Joe sits in crumpled despair

Angela enters R

Angela (*putting her head in at the door*) *You* haven't seen Millicent, have
you?

Joe shakes his head lifelessly

Paul wants her for something, that's all. (*She withdraws looking queerly at
Joe*)

*Angela exits R. Joe sits a moment longer, staring blankly. Then he gets to
his feet, absently takes out the piece of paper with notes, looks at it, sighs,
tears it up, looks vaguely round for somewhere to put the pieces; finally
deposits them in his pocket and goes slowly up to the door up RC. Here his
manner suddenly changes. He halts. A look of angry determination comes
into his face. He opens the door and goes purposefully out and off L. He
leaves the door open. There is a slight pause. Pam enters R*

Pam (*putting her head in at the door*) I'll be back in a min—— (*She breaks
off*) Oh!

*Pam comes right in, looks round the room, sees the open door, goes up to it,
looks out, closes it, pauses, looking anxiously thoughtful, then hurries out
again R. There is a slight pause. Millicent enters up RC from off L. Sadly
romantic, she wanders down L, picks up her work-basket, carries it to the
chesterfield, sits and begins listlessly to put it in order. Paul enters up RC
from off R. He halts on seeing Millicent and a look of grim triumph comes
into his face. For a moment he looks at her unsuspecting back-view, then he
braces himself, turns and switches off the lights. The room is illuminated
only by the reading lamp on the buffet*

Millicent (*turning in surprise and seeing Paul*) What's that for?
Paul That's to spare your blushes. (*He crosses to LC*)
Millicent (*uncomprehendingly*) I beg your pardon?
Paul You see—I've got something to say which you might prefer to hear in
a bad light.
Millicent Something to . . .? (*She breaks off*)
Paul Yes. I've been looking for you since you said goodbye. It brought
things to a head.

Millicent (*bewildered*) I—I don't think I . . . (*She breaks off*)
Paul (*assuming a furtively sinister manner*) The things you said to me last week!
Millicent (*in growing dismay*) Oh, no!
Paul You can't say things like that to a man of *my* temperament, you know—and expect them to be forgotten. (*He moves in towards the* L *arm of the chesterfield*)
Millicent (*horrified*) You don't *mean* that? You don't *really* mean it?
Paul (*very unpleasant*) You can't dangle visions of rapture before *my* eyes, and then just snatch them away again, you know.
Millicent But, how can you *say* such things? I never dangled anything re*mo*tely re*sem*bling rapture. I never meant *any* of it *any*way. You *know* I didn't.
Paul (*slimily*) *Half* of you meant it. (*He begins very slowly to approach her*)
Millicent No!
Paul The *prim*itive half of you meant it.
Millicent I haven't got a pr——
Paul (*interrupting*) Oh, yes, you have! Those sultry eyes! That luscious mouth!
Millicent I don't think I can *quite* believe my ears.
Paul (*moving steadily closer behind the chesterfield and becoming steadily more offensive*) That warm, supple, *in*dolent body!

Millicent, in mounting terror, cringes against the L *end of the chesterfield*

Millicent (*trying to show a little spirit*) How *dare* you come in here talking about my body?
Paul (*leaning over and putting on a horrible leer*) Let me help you with your art.
Millicent (*recoiling in horror*) Oh, you *aw*ful old man!
Paul "Seasoned", I think, was the word. (*He moves round the* L *end of the chesterfield*) Let me add a little seasoning to your life.
Millicent (*rising and backing to* R, *keeping the chesterfield between them*) Oh, you dis*gust*ing old person, you!
Paul (*making sinister beckoning motions*) Come! (*He moves below the chesterfield to* R)
Millicent Oh, and to think that I . . . (*She moves above the chesterfield*)
Paul (*interrupting*) Come! To please Peter! (*He begins to move round the* R *end of the chesterfield*)
Millicent (*in panic*) Go away! Go away! (*She turns and runs for the shelter of the easy chair*)
Paul Ah! That's the other half talking now—the namby-pamby half. (*Following*) We'll soon break that down, won't we? (*He makes a sudden quick movement to the chair*)
Millicent (*circling the chair*) No!
Paul (*circling chair*) Come now, come! Let nature take its course.
Millicent (*backing to the fireplace*) Don't you come over here!
Paul (*advancing; beckoning horribly*) Come!
Millicent (*with her back against the fireplace*) Keep away! I warn you. Keep away!

Paul (*advancing; beckoning*) Come!

Millicent opens her mouth and lets out a prolonged scream. Paul starts violently, stops in his tracks and glances at the door R. *His manner reverts abruptly to normal*

Paul (*nervously irate*) What did you do that for, you silly little fool? D'you want the whole place in here?
Millicent (*loudly*) Yes!
Paul (*appalled at the violence of Millicent's reaction*) You don't think I was *really* going to do anything, do you? (*He takes a step towards her*) Come away from . . .

Millicent, still flattened against the fireplace, screams again

(*Glancing anxiously at the door*) Shut up, for *heaven's* sake! (*He makes tracks for the door up* RC) It's not worth all that noise anyway. (*He turns and takes a step towards her, shaking his finger at her*) Another time, perhaps you'll think twice before you start . . .

Millicent screams again

Paul leaves with undignified haste, through the door up RC *and goes off* R. *Charles enters* R. *His sleeves are now rolled up and his hands and forearms blackened*

Charles (*entering precipitately*) What's up? What's up?

Angela enters R

Angela What's the *matter*?
Millicent (*leaving the fireplace and tottering towards Angela*) Oh, that revolting old creature!
Angela (*hurrying to Millicent at* LC) What?

Pam enters R *followed by Mrs Mandrake*

Pam What's happened? (*She crosses to the door up* RC *and switches on the lights*)
Millicent On, that rev——
Angela (*interrupting; very concerned*) *Which* revolting old creature, darling?
Millicent (*pointing at door up* RC) Him! He attacked me.
Angela Who did? (*She puts her arms protectingly round Millicent*)
Charles Paul?
Millicent Yes!
Pam (*losing interest*) Oh, that!
Angela Attacked you? What with?
Charles (*horrified*) You mean he . . .?
Millicent Yes!
Mrs Mandrake (*with satisfaction*) There you are!
Charles Where *is* the swine? Which way did he go?

Charles rushes out up RC *and off* R

Millicent sinks into the easy chair. Angela and Mrs Mandrake group round her

Angela (L *of the chair; incredulously*) Are you *sure* it was *Paul?*
Millicent Of *course* I'm sure.
Angela (*very disturbed*) But it seems so un*like* him.
Mrs Mandrake (R *of the chair*) Don't say *I* didn't warn you!
Angela (*to Millicent*) I've never *known* him do a thing like that, dear.
Millicent (*getting more coherent but beginning to snivel*) I can't see why that should be any comfort to *me.*
Mrs Mandrake (*to Angela*) You don't know *what* he's been doing for the past sixteen years.
Pam (*coming down* C; *impatiently*) Millicent, how *can* you make such a spectacle of yourself?
Millicent (*pathetically resentful*) *Me?*
Pam Yes. All this fuss about nothing!
Millicent You wait till *you* get chased round the furniture.
Angela Perhaps you mistook his intentions, dear.
Millicent Well, he had a funny way of going about it if he only wanted a game of dominoes.
Mrs Mandrake (*morbidly*) Did he make suggestions?
Millicent They were more like ultimatums.
Pam Well, what about it? Did *he* scream the house down when *you* made suggestions to *him?*
Millicent That was *entirely* different. I didn't *mean* it, for one thing.

Angela and Mrs Mandrake look rather bewildered

Pam He didn't *know* you didn't mean it. How do you know *he* meant it, anyway?
Millicent I wasn't going to stand there and find out.

Pam crosses to the fireplace

Angela (*kindly*) No, dear, of course you weren't. (*Urging Millicent out of the chair*) Now, you go with Mandy. She'll look after you.

Millicent rises. Mrs Mandrake puts an arm about her waist and conducts her towards the door R

(*Very disturbed*) What could he have been *think*ing of? (*She moves to* LC)
Mrs Mandrake (*at the door; quite severely*) I hope you don't expect anyone *here* to answer that question.

Mrs Mandrake and Millicent go out R

Angela What makes you think he mightn't have meant anything by it?
Pam The simple fact that he told Joe he was going to *do* it.
Angela (*astounded*) *Told Joe* he was going to do *that?*
Pam Well—something of the kind.
Angela Then he *did* mean it?
Pam (*patiently*) Mummy, if you *really* intend to—you don't say "excuse me a minute while I go and assault somebody".
Angela No, I suppose you don't. But *why* on *earth* . . .?
Pam (*interrupting*) To teach her a lesson.
Angela To . . .! *What?*

Pam For something she'd *done* to him. He was an*noy*ed.
Angela *Oh, I see! (It is doubtful whether she really does see, but she is very ready to be convinced)* He was an*noy*ed—*not* amorous.—Well, I do think he might have made that clear to the child.

Paul enters up RC *from off* R. *He is sniffing and dabbing at his nose with a bloody handkerchief. Shutting the door he strides straight down to the door* R

Angela *(horrified)* Paul!
Paul *(violently)* Go to hell!
Angela *(shocked)* Paul!
Paul *(pausing at the door and indicating the garden)* That chap's too good for *you.*

Paul exits R

Angela *(in astonishment)* He's hit him. Charles has hit him.

Angela and Pam both turn and run to the door up RC, *where they stand looking out*

Can you see anything?
Pam What's that—*(pointing)* over there?
Angela *(calling)* Charles—is that you—in the rose bed, dear?

Silence for a moment

I'll see if I can find him. You go and help your father with his nose.

Pam runs off R

Angela comes down to the chesterfield, snatches up Charles' jacket and turns to the door

Charles enters up RC *from off* R. *Charles also holds a bloody handkerchief to his nose. There is a smear of blood across his face. He is out of breath and unsteady on his feet, but he carries himself with an air of triumph*

Angela *(moving up to meet him)* Charles!
Charles *(breathlessly)* Well—*(he sniffs)* that'll teach him. *(Sniff)*
Angela What *have* you been doing? *(She shuts the door)*
Charles Sorry it had to come to this, old girl, but *(he sniffs)* when a feller . . .
Angela *(interrupting)* Do try not to bleed on the carpet, dear! Here—sit down!

She pilots Charles towards LC. *As he comes from the shelter of the chesterfield we see his trouser leg is torn. Angela sits him in the easy chair*

Charles *(sitting)* When a feller . . . *(Sniff)*
Angela *(interrupting)* That's right! Now put your head back!

Charles complies

I'll get a key or something. *(She starts towards* R)
Charles No, no, don't bother! It's stopping now.

Angela Charles, you shouldn't *do* this sort of thing at your time of . . . (*she checks herself*) at—er—this time of night.

Charles Oh, I'm all right. Don't worry about me. Matter of fact, it's (*he sniffs*) done me a lot of good.

Angela (*doubtfully*) One wouldn't say so, dear, to look at you.

Charles No, I mean psychologically. (*He hesitates*) You see . . . (*He breaks off*)

Angela Yes?

Charles (*in a burst of confidence*) I *must* tell you this, Angela. It's really rather funny. (*He sniffs*) Fact is, I've been getting a bit worried.

Angela (*concerned*) Worried, dear?

Charles Yes. (*He sniffs*) This feller Paul's been making quite an impression on me.

Angela Is that something to worry about?

Charles Well, you see—I'd rather expected to be able to detect something about him that would account for your—er—your inability to live with him.

Angela (*keenly interested*) Oh!

Charles But, I *couldn't*! (*He laughs rather self-consciously*) In fact, as time went on, he impressed me more and more as a decent chap.

Angela (*who seems almost to be leading him on*) Yes?

Charles So naturally I began to think—*well* (*he laughs*)—if a woman can't get on with a chap like that—perhaps, after all, there's—er . . .

Angela (*interposing*) Something wrong with the woman!

Charles (*laughing uncomfortably*) Well, I wouldn't put it as strongly as that. But you know what I mean. (*He dabs at his nose*)

Angela But, of course! It's most excellent logic, Charles. Do you think it's broken?

Charles Feels as if it's pulped. So, what with one thing and another, I must confess I was ex*tremely* relieved when he made this dastardly attempt and showed himself up, once and for all, as the sort of outsider that no decent woman could live with.

Angela I see.

Charles Well, it's all right *now* (*he laughs*)—in fact, it's quite amusing, but . . . (*He breaks off laughing and shakes his head in rueful recollection*)

Angela (*unsmilingly*) Yes, it's very funny, dear. There's only *one* thing . . .! (*She moves behind the easy chair*)

Charles (*still chuckling*) What?

Angela (*quite apologetically*) Well, I'm terribly sorry to have to tell you this—but there hasn't *been* any dastardly attempt.

Charles (*not taking it in*) How d'you mean?

Angela (*coming down* L *of the easy chair*) Apparently it was just some sort of misunderstanding.

Charles I don't think I follow.

Angela You see, dear, we cleared it all up when you were in the garden, hitting him.

Charles (*sitting forward*) Are you trying to tell me that he *did*n't attack the girl at *all*?

Angela I know it's an awful pity, but . . .

Charles (*interrupting resentfully*) How can you possibly have a misunderstanding over a thing like that?

Angela Well, you see—what Millicent mistook for erotic frenzy was apparently nothing more than annoyance. Silly of her, of course, but I dare say it's not always easy for an inexperienced girl to tell the difference.

There is a pause. Charles seems quite stunned. Angela looks very solemn

Charles So I punched him on the nose for nothing!

Angela I'm afraid so, dear.

Charles And got punched on the nose myself!

Angela (*regretfully*) Yes.

There is another short pause during which Charles is apparently realizing the implications of the situation

Charles And what's more—he's *still* a decent *chap*. (*He looks up at Angela*)

Angela (*smiling diffidently*) It *does* make things rather awkward now, doesn't it? (*She comes down to the fireplace*)

Pam enters R

Pam (*putting her head round the door*) I can't get at him. He's locked his door.

Angela (*crossing to* c) Well, don't come in here for a minute, darling! Go and comfort Millicent, or something!

Pam I've tried, but she won't *be* comforted.

Angela Go and make the tea, then!

Pam (*looking with morbid interest at Charles*) Good Lord! Hah!

Pam laughs shortly and exits R

Charles casts a resentful glance after Pam. There is an uncomfortable pause

Charles (*rising slowly*) Doesn't seem to be much to say after that, does there?

Angela (*subdued*) No, Charles!

Charles (*ruefully*) Bit of a giveaway, wasn't it?

Angela (*kindly*) Put your coat on, dear! (*She holds it up for him*)

Charles climbs into his jacket, then faces her

Charles (*sadly*) You know, Angela—I don't think I ever really believed it would come to anything.

Angela (*sadly*) I don't think I did, either.

Charles Perhaps I'm a bit—set in my ways to start thinking of that sort of thing.

Angela I expect we both are, dear.

Charles Well—anyway . . .! (*He smiles bravely*) Goodbye, Angela! (*He holds out his hand*)

Angela (*becoming affected*) You'll have a cup of tea before you go, won't you?

They shake hands

Charles No—I'll just slide out. (*He moves to the doors* L)

Angela (*following him; emotionally*) *Dear* Charles! (*She kisses him*) I do hope you like Peru.

Charles smiles, turns to the doors and hesitates

Charles There's just one last thing I—wish you'd get somebody to do for me. I don't think I could face it myself.
Angela (*gulping*) Anything, dear!
Charles Tell the vicar!
Angela (*in a half-whisper*) Yes.
Charles And Mr Atkins?

Angela, too overcome to answer, nods. Charles opens the door and looks at her a moment with deep affection

(*Sadly*) It's a pity, though—in a way.

Charles turns and exits through the porch, sniffing and dabbing at his nose. He shuts the door

Angela stands for a moment gazing after him, then she dabs her eyes, sighs, and moves to the L arm of the chesterfield and sits

Millicent enters R. A hat is stuck on the back of her head and she is struggling into an outdoor coat. At the same time she lugs a suitcase, from the lid of which underclothing protrudes

Millicent (*crossing below the chesterfield to C; rather breathlessly*) I've just thrown a few things into this. Perhaps Mandy 'ud kindly send on . . .
Angela (*rising; interrupting in surprise*) Are you going?
Millicent Yes, if you don't mind, I think I . . . (*She moves up* C)
Angela (*interrupting*) You *do* know you got it all wrong, don't you?
Millicent So Pam says—but I think I should feel safer, somehow, if . . . (*She breaks off*)
Angela Very well, dear!
Millicent (*dumping her suitcase on to the steadily growing pile of luggage by the piano and going to the desk*) May I ring for a car, please?
Angela Of course.
Millicent (*picking up the receiver*) Ilcombe two-four! (*She waits*) Red Lion? . . . Is that Mr Atkins? . . . Oh, Mr Atkins, I know it's late, but . . .

Paul enters R He carries a hat, raincoat and suitcase, and still looks very angry

Angela rises. Millicent stands transfixed with the receiver in her hand. Paul strides straight across up stage towards the luggage by the piano

Angela (*with a note of alarm*) Paul—what are you doing?
Paul Getting out! What do you think?
Angela (*anxiously*) Has anything happened?
Paul (*loudly and angrily*) Has anything *happ*ened! Are you all stark, staring crazy in this place? (*He planks his suitcase on the pile beside Millicent's and begins putting on his coat*)
Angela But Paul—we're not annoyed with you about that. We *know* it was only a muddle.

Paul What you don't seem to appreciate is that it's not a question of you being annoyed with me.

Angela No?

Paul No. It's *me* being annoyed with *you*.

Angela (*slightly affronted*) Oh!

Paul (*to Millicent*) Do you mind if I ring for a car when you've finished fiddling with that?

Millicent jumps nervously and replaces receiver

Angela (*coldly*) Millicent *was* ringing for a car.

Paul Right! Well, we'll share it.

Millicent Oh, no, we won't. (*She backs down* L *away from Paul*) Mrs Dickson—if he's going to be on the train, *I'm* going to *stay*. (*She stands with her back to the fire*)

Angela (*to Paul*) May I ask what you have to be annoyed about?

Paul (*bitterly sarcastic*) Well, of course, I may be getting touchy, but (*he goes to the desk*) I don't much like having my temptations ar*ranged* for me, that's all. (*He picks up the phone*)

Angela I haven't the re*mot*est idea what you're talking about.

Paul (*into the phone*) Ilcombe—er—(*to Angela*) what is it?

Angela (*irritably*) Two-four!

Paul (*into the phone; irritably*) Two-four. (*To Angela*) First you get up a plot to disgrace me in the eyes of my daughter—then you put out a remarkably ripe piece of cheese as ground-bait—then you ... (*Into the phone*) Hullo! Mr Atkins?

Angela (*indignantly*) *What* piece of cheese?

Millicent (*timidly*) I think he means me.

Paul		(*into the phone*) I'm speaking from Mrs Dickson's house. ... What?
	}(*together*){	
Angela		(*to Millicent*) Do *you* know what he's talking about?

Millicent Yes, I ...

Paul (*interrupting irritably*) Quiet—please! I can't hear a w—— (*Into the phone*) Yes?

Millicent *She* didn't know anything about it, Mr Dickson.

Paul (*into the phone*) No, this is ... (*To Millicent*) What did you say?

Millicent It was nothing to do with *her*.

Paul Nothing to ... (*He breaks off*)

Millicent No. It was only *my* idea.

Paul And—and she ...? (*He breaks off, indicating Angela*)

Millicent No!

Paul (*deflating*) Oh! (*He sits on the stool, nonplussed, holding the receiver*)

There is a slight pause. Angela, looking smug, comes down and seats herself in the chesterfield. Millicent stands irresolute

Millicent (*crossing to* C) Well—I think I'll go to bed.

Angela Yes, dear, I think I should.

Millicent moves up to the luggage, abstractedly picks up Paul's suitcase, hesitates and turns to Paul

Millicent I'm—I'm sorry if I . . .
Paul That's mine, anyway.
Millicent Oh!

Millicent hurriedly interchanges the suitcases, rushes across to the door R *and exits*

Paul (*suddenly remembering the phone and lifting it to his ear*) Hullo! . . . Damn, he's cut off! (*Irritably*) What's the matter with these fellows? Don't they *want* custom? (*He starts jiggling the receiver rest—then gruffly*) I'm sorry, Angela! I was misinformed.
Angela (*smugly*) That's all right, dear.
Paul (*into the phone*) Ilcombe . . . (*He looks enquiringly at Angela*)
Angela (*sweetly*) Two-four!
Paul (*into the phone; sweetly*) Two-four!
Angela While you're about it, Paul—would you mind telling Mr Atkins that we shan't want the car to-morrow, after all?
Paul (*absently*) Uh-huh!
Angela And that there won't be any reception?
Paul Right! No car and no rec—— (*Looking up; startled*) What? Why not?
Angela We've . . . Charles and I have . . . (*She breaks off*)
Paul (*placing the receiver on the stool*) You've broken it off?

Angela nods. Paul rises slowly

(*After a slight pause*) I say—I'm awfully sorry to hear that. (*He begins to take off his coat*) What happened?
Angela Charles was afraid he mightn't be able to put up with me.
Paul Silly ass! (*He throws his coat over the back of the easy chair*)
Angela (*with a sad little smile*) *You* couldn't, Paul.
Paul That's entirely different. I was young, impetuous, hot-headed.
Angela You think Charles has had time to learn patience?
Paul (*crossing to the chesterfield*) I'm sure *I* have.
Angela (*gently*) *Have* you, Paul?
Paul Of course! We all do. (*He sits beside her on her* L) Have you ever realized what stupid, trivial little things we used to quarrel about?
Angela Indeed I have. (*She smiles*) Only last night I was thinking of the time I went to mother for a fortnight simply because you insisted that *In a Monastery Garden* was by Sibelius.

They both laugh

Paul Well, there you are. D'you think we could make such fools of ourselves *now*?

Angela does not reply, but sits with downcast eyes

(*Earnestly*) Angela—has it ever occurred to you that there never *were* any *real* differences between us? Doesn't it seem rather a pity that . . . (*He breaks off*)

Pam enters R. *She bears a tray of tea-things*

Pam (*in pleased surprise at seeing Angela and Paul sitting amicably together*) Oh!

Angela Ah! Blessed tea!

Paul Can I give you a hand?

Pam (*coming in front of the chesterfield*) No, thanks. Charles gone? (*She hands the tray to Angela and goes up to* C *to the piano for the occasional table*)

Angela Er—yes, dear.

Pam brings the table down C

Joe bursts in up RC *from off* L. *There is a rather wild look in his eye*

Angela (*in surprise*) Joe!

Joe (*coming down* C) Sorry, Mrs Dickson, but—can I talk to Pam?

Pam puts the occasional table in front of Angela

Angela (*placing the tray on the table*) Certainly, dear! D'you want to—er . . . (*She breaks off discreetly*)

Joe (*loudly, positively and a little defiantly*) No. I don't care *who* hears it.

They all look at him in surprise

Pam What's the matter with you?

Joe (*aggressively*) I've got my car outside. Are you going to elope with me or aren't you?

Pam What are you talking about?

Joe (*crossing below the chesterfield to* R) You know perfectly well what I'm talking about, and I don't want to mess about over it all night, either. I want a straight answer one way or the other. Are you or aren't you? (*He moves up* R *of the chesterfield*)

Pam Well, of course I'm not. (*She begins dispensing tea*)

Joe (*moving down* R; *appealing to the others*) There you are, you see! She said herself . . .

Pam (*interrupting*) I didn't say at this time of night.

Angela We're just going to bed, dear.

Pam You can't *get* married after six o'clock, anyway. (*She moves round the table so that her back is towards Joe*)

Joe We can keep on driving all night, then.

Angela But it 'ud have to be in the parish where your banns were read.

Joe (*wildly*) All right! We'll drive round in *circles*.

Pam (*pouring tea*) Don't be silly, Joe!

Joe (*warningly*) It's your last chance, you know.

Pam (*quite kindly*) Come back in the morning, dear—when you've slept it off a bit. (*She is bending over the tray. Her behind, with slacks stretched tightly over it, is presented invitingly towards Joe*)

Joe's eyes fix on to it in a fascinated way

Joe (*darkly*) You said yourself, you needed a firm hand. (*He draws up his right sleeve slightly*)

Pam (*to Angela*) I'll get some hot water.

Pam runs off R

Angela (*to Joe*) Have a cup of tea, dear!

Joe (*ignoring this; staring after Pam*) I don't know about you, Mr Dickson—but *I* think there's only one thing that'll do that girl any good!

Paul (*who has observed the scene with mild and placid interest; regretfully*) She's too big for *me* to give it to her, Joe.

Joe hesitates momentarily, then, turning up his cuff, follows firmly after Pam, and exits R

Angela (*innocently*) What is she too big for you to . . .?

Paul (*interrupting hurriedly; handing her his cup*) Got any more tea? (*He casts an uneasy glance at the door and continues*) Erm—do you remember the way we used to sit over our tea at night, Angela, discussing all the little incidents of the day?

Angela (*starting to re-fill his cup*) Yes, dear, but what . . .? (*She breaks off*)

Pam (*off*) *Joe!* What are you *doing?*

Angela and Paul sit up listening. Angela a little startled, Paul with a certain dread

   Joe!

Paul (*loudly*) Do you remember . . .? (*He breaks off*)

Two loud slapping noises are heard off R

Pam (*off*) Ow! *Stop* it! *Ow!*

Angela (*relaxing in relief*) Oh, bless them! They've made it up. They're fooling. (*She goes on placidly pouring out Paul's tea*)

Four more slaps are heard off R. *Paul flinches visibly at each yelp from Pam*

Pam (*off*) Ow! Ow! Ow! Ow!

Angela (*indulgently*) *Are*n't they naughty? (*She hands Paul his cup*) What were you saying, dear?

Paul (*rather shaken; lamely*) I—er—I think I was saying something about the way we used to sit over our tea.

Angela Oh, yes! Paul, do you remember the Dream Book?

Paul The . . .? Yes indeed!

Angela I still have it. (*Rising and hurrying across to the desk*) I turned it out the other day when I was packing. (*She opens a drawer of the desk and takes out the book*)

Joe enters R. *He walks, slowly, like a man with a great sorrow, straight across to the doors* L

Angela and Paul watch him in silence

Joe (*at the doors; apathetically*) Good-night!

Joe exits through the porch

Angela You know—sometimes I think that boy's a little strange in his manner. (*She at once dismisses the thought and bears the book down to Paul*) Look!

Paul eases along the chesterfield towards C. *Angela stands on his* L

Paul (*taking the book*) Good Lord! The old Dream Book! Well, well, well!

Angela What *fun* we used to have with such *silly* things, Paul!
Pam (*off; calling, distantly*) Joe!
Angela (*with a note of irritation*) What's the matter *now*?
Pam (*off; calling, closer*) Joe!

Pam enters R. *She is carrying her suitcase; she bursts in and rushes straight across towards* L

Paul and Angela watch in silent amazement

(*As she crosses; frantically*) Oh, *stop* him, somebody! *Joe!* (*She drops the suitcase half-way across and continues to the doors* L) *Joe!*

Paul rises wonderingly

(*She opens the doors* L *and shouts outside*) *Joe! Wait* for me! I'm coming. *Yes,* I'm coming. (*She turns, dashes down to Angela and throws her arms about her*) Goodbye, Mummy darling!

Angela seems too astounded to reply

I do hope you'll be happy. I don't think you will be, but I hope you are. (*She kisses her*) Goodbye!
Paul Aren't you coming back in the morning?
Pam (*with a delighted laugh*) Oh yes, of *course*! I'd forgotten about getting married. (*She grabs Paul's coat from the easy chair*) May I take this?
Paul Take it! Take it!

Pam begins to struggle into the coat

Angela Er—will you be seeing the vicar first thing then, dear?
Pam Yes.
Angela (*a little haltingly*) Well—while you're about it—would you mind telling him that—erm ... (*She hesitates*)
Pam (*interposing in delight*) You're *not* going to—after *all*?
Angela (*looking rather sheepish*) No, dear!
Pam Oh, *Mummy*! (*She flings herself on Angela and embraces her again, then turns and seizes Paul*) Oh, *Paul*, I'm so glad! (*She kisses him, turns away, picks up the suitcase and indicates it*) You see? I *knew* I was right in keeping it ready. (*She runs to the doors* L)
Angela I don't see why you *want* it if you're going to drive all night and are coming back in the ...
Pam (*at the doors, as if beginning an argument*) But *Mum*my, this is an el*ope*ment. You can't *poss*ibly ...

Joe appears at the open door, seizes her arm and jerks her violently off stage. They go off through the porch

Angela (*staring emotionally after Pam*) She didn't get the hot water after all, did she? (*She moves up to the doors* L *and closes them*)
Paul (*moving up to Angela*) There's nothing to be sad about, Angela. *They*'re all right! They're both good kids. (*He puts a comforting arm about her and impels her gently back to the chesterfield*)
Angela (*miserably*) So were we good kids.
Paul I know, dear.

They sit side by side

(*Briskly*) Now—what were we talking about?

Angela (*indicating the book still in Paul's hand*) That, I think.

Paul Oh yes—the old Dream Book! (*He opens it*) I wonder what it means to dream about a dog.

Angela Is that what you did?

Paul Yes—this afternoon—after lunch. (*Turning the pages*) Dog, dog, dog, dog!

Angela What sort of a dog was it?

Paul Oh, I don't know. Just an indiscriminate sort of dog—you know—brown eyes.

Angela Ahoouh! How sweet!

Paul (*finding the place*) Ah! "Dogs"!

Angela What was it doing, Paul?

Paul (*looking at the book*) Just following me, I think.

Angela D'you think it wanted something?

Paul (*half preoccupied with the book*) I don't know.

Angela (*struck by an awful thought*) Perhaps it was hungry!

Paul (*absently*) Perhaps!

Angela Well—didn't you try to find out?

Paul (*looking up*) How was *I* to find out?

Angela You could have offered it something to *eat*.

Paul I don't go around with dog-biscuits in my pocket.

Angela You could have gone into a shop and *bought* some, couldn't you?

Paul I didn't think of going into a shop, I suppose.

Angela Well, *I* think you *ought* to have thought of it.

Paul Oh, you do?

Angela Yes, I do.

Paul But, damn it, woman—this was a *dream*!

Angela I *know* it was a dream. That's not the *point*. It's the *prin*ciple of the thing!

Paul (*slamming the book and throwing it down; rising wildly*) Oh, for *hea*ven's *sake*! (*He crosses to* LC)

Angela It's no good getting excited about it, Paul. You know quite well that if there's *one* thing ...

Paul (*interrupting; waving his arms*) *All* I do is ...

Angela (*interrupting*) If there's one thing I can't *bear*, it's ...

Paul (*interrupting*) All I do is dream about a dog, and what happens?

Angela (*overlapping from "dream"*) If there's one thing I can't *bear*, it's *cruelty* to animals.

CURTAIN

FURNITURE AND PROPERTY LIST

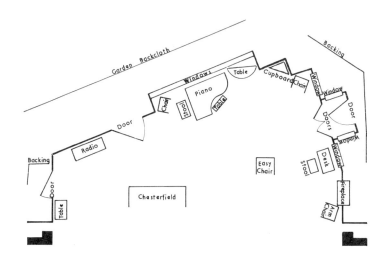

ACT I

On stage: Buffet, down R. *On it:* silver tray, 3 tumblers, soda syphon, bottle of
whisky, bottle of gin, sherry, ashtray, table lamp, handbag

Radiogram, up R. *On it:* bowl of flowers

Tall backed chair, in window. *On it:* Red hat

Piano stool

Piano, up C. *On it:* table lamp, vase of flowers, ashtray, 2 wooden book
troughs, 3 pairs of book ends, 8 toast racks, 4 blue enamel brushes,
blue enamel mirror, pair of brass candlesticks, cruet, silver sweet dish,
silver wine cooler, silver cigarette box, pair of sugar tongs, 2 jam
dishes, sugar basin

Low coffee table, under piano

Tall backed chair, by window up L

Desk, L. *On it:* telephone (no dial), blotter, ashtray, inkstand, pens,
pencils, table lamp, cigarette box (filled), bowl of flowers, shoe

Stool, at desk

Waste-paper basket, below desk

Small armchair, down L. *In it:* cushion

Easy chair, LC. *In it:* cushion, large piece of brown packing paper, piece
of thick string on R arm, compact

Chesterfield. *On it:* 4 cushions, large shabby suitcase, copies of *Woman
and Home* and *Men Only* and other magazines at L end, 2 dresses and
scarf (over the back)

Clock, on wall down R
2 Wall brackets, over mantelpiece
Fender, fire-irons, dogs, grate
Log basket, in fireplace
On mantelpiece: telegram in envelope, 2 brass candlesticks, 2 brass pots
On floor below easy chair: 4 empty cardboard boxes, odd pieces of string,
    12 pieces of coloured and tissue paper
On front door, off L: knocker
Curtains, on all windows
Light switch, L of door up RC
Long carpet, set parallel with back wall
3 Mats, in front of fire and door R and in porch

Off stage R: Pail, mop **(Mrs Coot)**
          Plunger **(Angela)**
          Prayer-book **(Pamela)**
          Carnation **(Charles)**

Off stage L: Cardboard box, wrapped, with toast rack **(Mrs Mandrake)**
          Telegram **(Pam)**
          Bridal bouquet **(Pam)**

ACT II

SCENE 1

Strike: All odd pieces of paper, string, boxes, dresses
          Toast rack on floor
          Bridal bouquet

Set: Carpet sweeper
          Prayer-book on piano, L
          Cigarette box (filled) on piano
          Magazines from L of chesterfield to R
          Piece of wrapping paper near armchair
          Piece of wrapping paper near suitcase
          Open door up RC

Off stage R: Apple **(Joe)**

Off stage L: Cardboard soap-box **(Paul)**
          Paper carrier-bag **(Angela)**
          Two-tier wedding cake **(Charles)**

SCENE 2

Strike: All wedding presents, carpet sweeper, all dirty glasses
          Close window
          Close all doors

Set: Prayer-book on piano
          Top-hat on piano
          Key in door up RC
          Turn easy chair slightly towards chesterfield

Off stage R: Encyclopædia **(Pam)**
Book of clothing coupons **(Mrs Mandrake)**

Personal: **Joe:** cigarettes and lighter
Pam: handkerchief

ACT III

Strike: Flowers on desk
Close all curtains

Set: Golf clubs on chesterfield, L end
Labels on desk
Work basket on floor by armchair down L
Dress on armchair down L
Paul's jacket over back of armchair down L
Charles' jacket on back of chesterfield, R end
2 large empty cardboard boxes on floor L of piano
Odd shoes and hats on piano
Dress over back of chesterfield
Dress on cardboard boxes
Hat on chair up R
Magazines on radiogram
Letters and bills on mantelpiece
Evening paper on chair up L
Dream Book in drawer of desk
Turn easy chair slightly towards fireplace
Change flowers on radiogram

Off stage R: Silver tea-set on tray ⎱ **(Pam)**
Coat and suitcase   ⎰
2 Large trunks **(Paul** and **Charles)**
Large suitcase, hat and coat **(Paul)**
Suitcase, bag, hat and coat **(Millicent)**
Bunch of keys **(Mrs Mandrake)**
Tea cloth   ⎱ **(Charles)**
Torn grey flannel trousers ⎰

Personal: **Joe:** piece of paper
Paul: bloodstained handkerchief, cigarettes, lighter
Charles: bloodstained handkerchief

LIGHTING PLOT

ACT I

No. 1 BATTEN; 1 circuit (*No. 54 Pale Rose*) On check.

FLOATS; 1 circuit (*Open White*), 1 circuit (*White Frost*) FULL.

No. 4 BATTEN and FLOODS on backcloth; (*Open White*) FULL.

SPOTS to cover; easy chair RC, buffet and door R, desk and stool L, chesterfield, piano stool, porch doors L, door up RC, fireplace and armchair down L, down stage C. (*Possible colours 54 Pale Rose, 51 Gold Tint, 52 Pale Gold, 36 Pink.*) As required.

PAGEANT LAMP; (*Open White*) off R directed through the R end of the window up C towards the porch doors L.

ACT II, SCENE 1

No. 1 BATTEN; out.

FLOATS; 1 circuit (*Open White*) on check, 1 circuit (*White Frost*) FULL.

No. 4 BATTEN and FLOODS on backcloth; as ACT I.

SPOTS; as ACT I.

PAGEANT LAMP; (*4 Amber*) set as ACT I.

SCENE 2

No. 1 BATTEN; circuit (*54 Pale Rose*) on check.

FLOATS; 1 circuit (*White Frost*) on check, 1 circuit (*54 Pale Rose*) FULL.

No. 4 BATTEN and FLOODS on backcloth; (*3 Straw*) FULL.

SPOTS; as ACT I. Except SPOTS covering buffet and desk which should be out for the opening of this scene.

PAGEANT LAMP; (*4 Amber*) off L directed through the L end of the window up C towards the buffet and door R. If available two more PAGEANT LAMPS should be directed through the windows above and below the porch doors L towards the door R and the chesterfield respectively.

Cue 1 **Angela** (*considering*): "Now what shall I need?"
Check to OUT in 10 minutes; No. 1 BATTEN, FLOATS.
Check to ¾ in 10 minutes; No. 4 BATTEN, and FLOODS, PAGEANT LAMPS.
Check SPOTS as required.

Cue 2 **Millicent** *switches on the lights*
Snap on; all FITTINGS, FLOATS 1 circuit (*54 Pale Rose*) FULL, SPOTS as required, including those covering buffet and desk.
Continue check of No. 4 BATTEN and FLOODS to ½ and PAGEANT LAMPS to ¼ in 3 minutes.

Cue 3 **Angela** *switches off the lights*
Snap off; all FITTINGS, SPOTS, PAGEANT LAMPS.
Check; FLOATS to ¼ No. 4 BATTEN and FLOODS to ¼.

Cue 4 **Angela** *switches on the lights*
Return to lighting immediately prior to *Cue* 3.

ACT III

No. 1 BATTEN; out.
FLOATS; 1 circuit (54 *Light Rose*) FULL.
FLOODS on backcloth outside door RC; (82 *Blue*) on check.
SPOTS; as ACT I.
All FITTINGS ON.

Cue 1 **Paul** *switches off the lights*
Snap off; FLOATS, all FITTINGS except lamp on buffet, all SPOTS except those covering chesterfield, buffet, and area down stage C.

Cue 2 **Pam** *switches on the lights*
Return to opening lighting.

GRAMOPHONE RECORDS USED

ACT I. CURTAIN . . . Wedding March Bells . . . Columbia YB.8.
ACT II, SCENE 2. CURTAIN . . . Queen's Chimes . . . Columbia DB.1637.

MADE AND PRINTED IN GREAT BRITAIN BY
LATIMER TREND & COMPANY LTD PLYMOUTH
MADE IN ENGLAND